# Did You Know?

# Did You Know

**500 Facts Revealed**

**Moumita Das**
**Chinmoy Kumar Ghosh**

Viva Books
New Delhi | Mumbai | Chennai | Kolkata
Bengaluru | Hyderabad | Kochi | Guwahati

**Publisher's note**

Every possible effort has been made to ensure that the information contained in this book is accurate at the time of going to press, and the publisher and authors cannot accept responsibility for any errors or omissions, however caused. No responsibility for loss or damage occasioned to any person acting, or refraining from action, as a result of the material in this publication can be accepted by the editor, the publisher or the authors.

Every effort has been made to trace the owners of copyright material used in this book. The authors and the publisher will be grateful for any omission brought to their notice for acknowledgment in the future editions of the book.



First Published 2013
Reprinted 2015, 2016, 2017, 2018, 2020, 2023

Viva Books Private Limited

- 4737/23, Ansari Road, Daryaganj, New Delhi 110 002
  Tel. 011-42242200, 23258325, 23283121, Email: vivadelhi@vivagroupindia.in
- 76, Service Industries, Shirvane, Sector 1, Nerul, Navi Mumbai 400 706
  Tel. 022-27721273, 27721274, Email: vivamumbai@vivagroupindia.in
- Megh Tower, Old No. 307, New No. 165, Poonamallee High Road, Maduravoyal, Chennai 600095
  Tel. 044-23780991, 23780992, Email: vivachennai@vivagroupindia.in
- B-103, Jindal Towers, 21/1A/3 Darga Road, Kolkata 700 017
  Tel. 033-22816713, Email: vivakolkata@vivagroupindia.in
- 7, GF, Sovereign Park Aptts., 56-58, K. R. Road, Basavanagudi, Bengaluru 560 004
  Tel. 080-26607409, Email: vivabangalore@vivagroupindia.in
- 101-102, Moghal Marc Apartments, 3-4-637 to 641, Narayanguda, Hyderabad 500 029 Tel. 040-27564481, Email: vivahyderabad@vivagroupindia.in
- First Floor, Beevi Towers, SRM Road, Kaloor, Kochi 682 018
  Tel. 0484-2403055, 2403056, Email: vivakochi@vivagroupindia.in
- 232, GNB Road, Beside UCO Bank, Silpukhuri, Guwahati 781 003
  Tel. 0361-2666386, Email: vivaguwahati@vivagroupindia.in

*www.vivagroupindia.com*

ISBN: 978-81-309-2430-4

Published by Viva Books Private Limited, 4737/23 Ansari Road, Daryaganj, New Delhi 110 002.

Printed and bound at Replika Press Pvt. Ltd.

X0000

Dedicated to

Our Parents

Bijoy Bhushan Das, Purnima Das

&

Late Ajit Kumar Ghosh, Late Shefali Ghosh

# Preface

Creativity is inherent in all of us. Creativity is the ability to generate ideas for products, services or processes that are new or those which never existed earlier. Creativity can be instrumental in devising innovative solutions for difficult problems. Therefore, creativity forms an integral part of any innovation process. It requires deviating from old methods and patterns of thinking and embracing new methods.

Creativity and innovativeness in an individual can be fostered among others through various methods, such as exploring creative interest, collecting inspiration, learning something new every day, and expanding the imagination. Considering the above aspects, we decided that a book that can stretch the imagination and inspire an individual to create and innovate would be timely.

The genesis of this book lies in a series of posters that we have been bringing out at the National Centre for Innovations in Distance Education at IGNOU, New Delhi. One rainy day in September 2010, we were apprehending that Delhi would get flooded after the Haryana Government released 7.7 lakh cusecs of water into the Yamuna. We asked a staff member if he knew what a 'cusec' was, and on receiving a reply in the negative, we explained it to him. We found that it was not only him but others also did not know what was meant by a 'cusec'. Similarly we found on 23$^{rd}$ September, 2010 that many did not know the significance of 'autumnal equinox', which normally falls on that day. These marked the starting point of a series of posters titled "Did You Know?"

Since then we have been working on sensitizing the general public about these interesting issues around us. These issues generally go unnoticed but they have a lot of bearing on our daily life. An awareness of the underlying reason for these issues or facts or phenomena could guide our everyday decisions and activities. For example, if a person is stung by a bee, and he or she knows that the sting of a bee is acidic, and therefore it can be neutralized with a compound of opposite nature, i.e., alkali, such as calcium hydroxide or slaked lime, which is easily available in a *paan* shop, it would be of enormous help to the person as a first aid.

We also chose facts which might not have direct bearing with our daily lives, but would have aroused the feeling that the information was worth knowing, like 'Abraham Lincoln and Charles Darwin were born on the same day, 12th February, 1809 at two different parts of the globe', or that, 'Every drop of seawater contains approximately 1 billion gold atoms'.

The compilation of the topics for this book required extensive research work, which involved referring to the authoritative texts, such as the encyclopedias, dictionaries, research articles, etc., for correct representation of the facts and figures. However, the task was enjoyable and highly exciting. We have purposefully not followed an ordered sequence but compiled the facts in a random fashion, with the aim to induce vibrancy of flow of thoughts in the mind of the reader. One of our objectives is to develop 'Questioning Skills' and we expect that our readers would raise pertinent questions.

Our exercise of displaying the posters was received with quite a significant element of enthusiasm. However, we are taking a leaf out of Tagore's book to make a reflection about the spirit behind this exercise. Here is our translation of an excerpt of a poem by Tagore.

*I have a desire to give you something*
*How does it matter even if you do not require it!*
*When we met, you were alone*
*Treading a path through a deep forest.*
*I felt the urge to light a lamp in order to show you the path*
*How does it matter even if you had not required it!*

We are grateful to our colleagues at the National Centre for Innovations in Distance Education, Indira Gandhi National Open University, New Delhi, for their cooperation. We would like to thank Viva Books Pvt. Ltd. for inspiring us by bringing this book out.

We hope that people from all walks of life, with curiosity and creativity, would find this book most interesting and useful. We shall be happy to receive comments from the readers through e-mail (moumitadas@yahoo.com; contactckg@gmail.com)

**Authors**

## The names of the three wise monkeys are Mizaru (See no evil), Kikazaru (Hear no evil), and Iwazaru (Say no evil)

The three wise monkeys were popularized in Japan and is believed to be part of the Chinese philosopher Confucius' teachings on the human code of conduct. These three monkeys depict the three principles of see no evil, hear no evil and speak no evil. Mizaru is depicted covering his eyes with his hands that symbolizes see no evil, Kikazaru is depicted covering his ears that symbolizes hear no evil and Iwazaru is depicted covering his mouth that symbolizes speak no evil. It is noteworthy that Mahatma Gandhi possessed a statue of these three monkeys. A larger statue of these monkeys is displayed at the Sabarmati Ashram in Ahmedabad, Gujarat.

## 'Cusec' means Cubic Foot per Second

Cusec is a method of measuring the flow rate of liquids. One cusec is 1 cubic foot per second. It means a volume of water 1 foot high, 1 foot wide and 1 foot long travelling a distance of 1 foot in 1 second. One cusec is equivalent to 0.028317 cubic metre per second. Mostly the cusec is applied in measuring the flow of liquid, such as flow of oil in pipelines, and especially the flow of water in the rivers and its quantum of release through barrages, dams, etc., during floods.

## Chalk is made of trillions of microscopic skeleton fossils of plankton

A plankton is a tiny organism found in the sea. A group of plankton named Coccolithophores comprises the chalk forming organisms. These organisms are microscopic and have shells made of lime. About 100 million years ago, during the Cretaceous period, these planktons settled down on the sea bed after death and formed lime mud. Subsequent layers of the skeletal remains of these organisms got added followed by the geological conditions of tremendous pressure and heat. This resulted in the formation of rocks, which we now known as chalk.

## Dragonflies are one of the fastest insects, flying 50 to 60 miles per hour or 80 to 96 km per hour

A dragonfly is a double winged insect with its forewings larger than the hind wings. When the dragonfly is at rest, the wings are held perpendicular to its body. These insects eat other small insects. Robert John Tillyard, while studying the genus *Austrophlebia,* found that the dragonfly could fly nearly at the rate of fifty miles (80 km) to sixty miles (96 km) an hour.

## The period 1920–1930 may be hailed as the 'golden era' of Physics in India when four important discoveries were made

In 1920, Meghnad Saha discovered his ionization formula (Saha Ionization Equation). In 1924, Satyendra Nath Bose found his photon derivation of Planck's Law (Bose Statistics). In 1928, Chandrasekhara Venkata Raman discovered the Raman Effect. In 1930, Subrahmanyan Chandrasekhar predicted the Chandrasekhar Limit. Together they contributed to the golden era of Indian physics.

## The only sport played on the moon is the 'Golf'

On 6th February 1971, Alan Shepard commanded the Apollo 14 mission and landed on the moon. Unknown to anyone, he had smuggled two golf balls and a club inside his spacesuit, and at the end of the day's moonwalk, he became the first man to hit a golf ball on the Moon. His thick gloves and a stiff spacesuit forced him to swing the club with only one hand. He hit two balls just before lift-off, and drove them, as he put it, 'miles and miles and miles'. The point to be noted is that the value of acceleration due to gravity on moon is one-sixth of that on earth.

## 'Waka Waka' has been scripted in the Cameroonian language Fang. It means 'Do it'

*Waka Waka* gained its popularity during the 2010 World Cup Football when Shakira sang the famous song. The lyrics of song contain words from the Fang language, which run as *Za mina mina eh eh Waka waka eh eh, Tsa mina mina zangalewa, this time for Africa. Za mina mina* means come, *Waka waka means* do it, *Tsa mina mina zangalewa means* where do you come from? Originally sung by a Makossa group from Cameroon called Golden Sounds, the band members comprised African soldiers. The song pays tribute to African infantry during World War II. During the Nigerian war (1967-70), the Nigerian army used this song extensively. The song is still used today almost everywhere in Africa.

## Gary Sobers did not know one important rule of cricket

In the 1971 Test match series against the West Indies, the first day of the first test match was washed out due to rains. India batted first and it turned out that India led by more than 150 runs in the first innings and there was only one day left. So the captain of Indian Team Ajit Wadekar went straight to the West Indies dressing room and asked Gary Sobers, captain of the West Indian team, 'Mr. Sobers would you like to bat?' He looked surprised and asked Wadekar whether he was enforcing the follow-on, and did he know the rules. There should be at least a 200-run deficit. Wadekar said, 'Perhaps you forgot to read further. It also says that in a match, which has been curtailed by a day from the very beginning, the deficit has to be at least a hundred and fifty runs.' Sobers still sat there in a state of shock and asked again: 'Are you sure?'

## The dot over the letter 'i' is called a 'tittle' (pronounced tid el lee)

Derived from the Latin word *titulus*, meaning inscription or heading, the tittle is a dot or diacritic that is used to mark a lowercase i or j. It was initially used to distinguish 'I' and 'J' from the neighbouring letters. The tittle appeared in the Latin alphabets in the $11^{th}$ century. Originally a larger mark, it was reduced to a dot in the later Roman letters. These days the word 'tittle' is rarely used and has been replaced with the word 'dot'.

## The time taken for a red blood cell to circle the whole body is 20 seconds

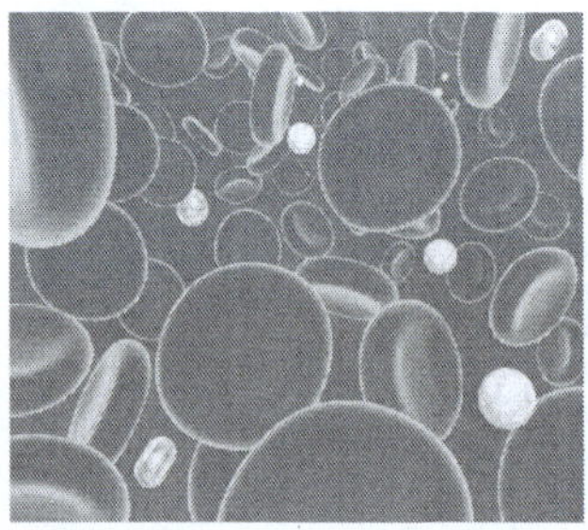

The red blood cells carry oxygen from the lungs to the different parts of the body. One trip takes the cell from the heart through the various blood vessels to the different parts of the body and back to the heart in 20 seconds. A red blood cell is estimated to live in the body for four months. They originate in the bone marrow and during their lifetime, they make 250,000 trips circumnavigating the body before returning to the bone marrow where they eventually die.

## In Venus the Sun rises in the West and sets in the East

Venus is the second planet from the sun in our solar system. It is the brightest object observed in the sky. Astronomers discovered that Venus moves clockwise as opposed to the counter-clockwise rotation of the earth. Therefore, it is said that in Venus the sun rises in the west and sets in the east.

## A group of owls is called a Parliament

The owl is believed to possess a wise disposition. Therefore a group of 'owls' is called a 'Parliament'. The word 'Parliament' is used as a collective noun in this case. Another collective noun for a group of owls is 'Wisdom of Owls'.

## The 'ZIP' in Zip Code stands for 'Zone Improvement Plan'

The Zone Improvement Plan Code, abbreviated as the ZIP Code is a system of postal codes that was introduced in the USA in 1963 to improve the efficiency of postal services, such as sorting and delivery. It comprises nine digits; the first three digits are assigned to a specific part of the USA, the next two digits refer to the specific post office or zone, the next two digits refer to a particular area or street or a cluster of buildings and the last two digits refer to a block or a single floor or a group of post office boxes, e.g., PO Box 58001, Washington DC 20037-8001.

## Mercury is the only metal that is liquid at room temperature

Mercury or quick silver is a metal, which is liquid. It has a very low melting point at minus 38.83 degrees celsius. It means that if the temperature falls below minus 38.83 degrees celsius, it will turn into solid. Under the conditions of room temperature, mercury is in liquid state.

## The astronauts' personal safety mascot is Snoopy from the Peanuts comics

Peanuts is a popular comics strip created by Charles M. Schulz. One of the main characters, Snoopy, a beagle, is the official mascot for the US astronauts. On January 27, 1967, the launch test for the Apollo 1 mission went wrong when the crew cabin caught fire killing all three astronauts on board. The Apollo Program was rebuilt with vigour and Snoopy became the official mascot of aerospace safety due to his attitude of refusal to accept defeat and his 'outside the doghouse' way of looking at things.

## Toothed whales eat fish and plants. They have only one nostril or blowhole

Whales are the world largest animals and are found in the oceans. Whales are mammals, which feed milk to their young ones and breathe air. Since they do not have gills they cannot breathe under water but have to come up to the surface of water to breathe. The air is breathed in and out through their 'blowhole,' which is on their back. There are two types of whales, baleen and toothed. The baleen whales do not have teeth, eat a plankton called krill and have two nostrils. The toothed whale eats plants and fishes and has only one nostril.

## The highest waterfalls in the world is the Angel Falls in Venezuela

The Angel Falls is located in the Venezuela. It is named after Jimmie Angel, a US aviator who was the first to fly over the falls in a plane. The waterfall has a height of 979 m, which is almost a kilometre. It is estimated that each drop of water takes 14 seconds to fall from the top to the bottom. Most interestingly, the origin of the waterfalls is not a river or any other water body like the other common waterfalls, but the rainfall from the clouds over the forests above the plateau from which the water falls.

## The infinity sign is called a 'lemniscate'

Infinity means something which does not have a limit. The infinity sign ∞ is called a lemniscate. The sign was devised by an English mathematician John Wallis in 1955 and was named lemniscus, meaning a 'pendant ribbon', by mathematician Jacob Bernoulli in 1694. The symbol is designed in two dimensions as a device known as the Möbius Strip (named after a 19th century mathematician August Ferdinand Möbius). A Möbius Strip is a strip of paper, which is twisted and attached at the ends, forming an 'endless' two dimensional surface.

## The word robot comes from the Czech word 'robotnik', which means forced labour or even slave

A robot is a machine that sometimes resembles humans and carries out routine mechanical tasks on command with human-like skill. The word Robot has its origins in the Czech word *Robotnik*, which means a serf or a slave. Robots are used mainly in factories and in those activities, which a human might find difficult to handle, such as deep sea exploration, mining, etc. It is also used in space.

## The first product to have a bar code was Wrigley's gum

The bar code was invented by Joseph Woodland and Bernard Silver in 1948. It was designed as a 'bulls eye' symbol comprising concentric circles. The initial idea of the bar code was to use it as a method for classifying grocery products. In 1970 a standard was set for all products and the Universal Grocery Products Identification Code (UGPIC) was written. It evolved further when in 1973 the Universal Product Code (UPC), which is currently in use, was invented by George J. Laurer. A scanner was installed in 1974 in Ohio and the first product to have a bar code was a 10 pack Wrigley's chewing gum.

## The word Google comes from the term 'Googol' which represents a number (written as a 1 followed by 100 zeros)

The term Googol was coined by 9-year-old Milton Sirotta, nephew of E. Kasner, an American mathematician. The creators of Google, Larry Page and Sergey Brin, wanted to name their search engine Googol as it symbolized their mission to cater millions of users. However, Googol was misspelt as Google and the name stuck.

## September 23 is the day of 'Autumnal Equinox'

The term 'equinox' is derived from the Latin *aequus* (equal) and *nox* (night). On this day the night and day are of the same length. This is because the tilt of the earth's axis is neither near nor away from the sun, and the centre of the sun and the centre of the earth are in the same plane. There are two equinoxes every year – one in September and another in March. The one in September is called the 'Autumnal Equinox' and the one in March is called the 'Spring Equinox'. The 'Spring Equinox' normally falls on March 21. The 'Autumnal Equinox' is observed in the northern hemisphere and marks the beginning of the autumn season. In Japan both equinoxes are observed as national holidays. In China around this time, the moon festival is observed, celebrating the abundance of summer's harvest.

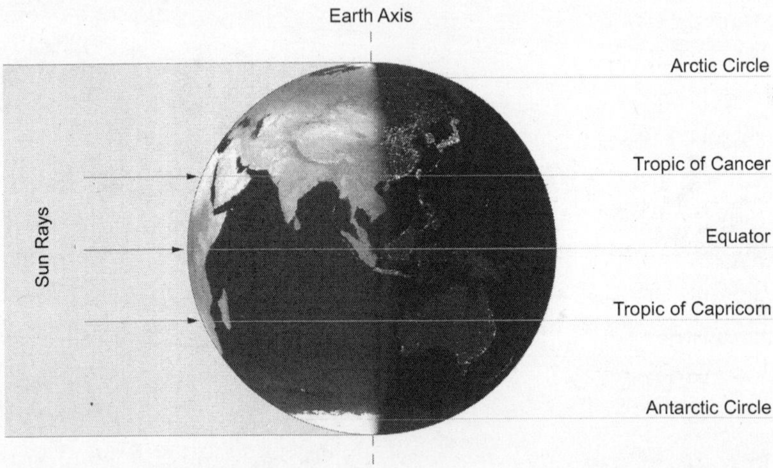


## The dinosaurs became extinct before the Rockies or the Alps were formed

The Rockies and Alps are fold mountains, which were formed due to the pushing up of the tectonic plates. This event happened about 30 to 40 million years ago. The dinosaurs roamed the Earth more than 65 million years ago, many million years before the existence of the Rockies or the Alps.

## Until the 19th century, solid blocks of tea were used as money in Tibet and Siberia

Tea bricks are made by compressing tea leaves of the black tea, ground tea or fermented variety. Because of its high value, tea bricks were used as currency in the late 19th and the 20th century in China and Tibet. Special tea bricks were made with ground tea leaves that were bound with flour or even blood and used as money. In Siberia, tea bricks were used as money as recently as around 1945.

## The plastic things on the end of shoelaces are called 'aglets'

The word 'aglet' is derived from old French word aguillette, which in turn originates from the Latin word *acus* meaning a needle. The aglets are plastic or metal sheaths that tightly cover the tips of shoelaces and cords to enable them to easily pass through the eyelet holes or other such lacing guides. In addition, the aglets keep the threads of a lace together and prevent them from fraying.

## The sum of a sequence of odd numbers gives you the sequence for perfect squares

$1 + 3 = 4$, $1 + 3 + 5 = 9$, $1 + 3 + 5 + 7 = 16$, $1 + 3 + 5 + 7 + 9 = 25$, $1 + 3 + 5 + 7 + 9 + 11 = 36$

## Rainforests higher than 3,000 feet above sea level are called 'cloud forests'

Cloud forests are usually found in the tropical or subtropical regions, such as South Africa, Indonesia and South America. They are also found in temperate regions, such as Japan and Pakistan. The clouds cover up to the middle level of these forests and persist there. The forests are dark due to low infiltration of light and the vegetation predominantly comprises ferns, orchids and mosses besides trees, such as pine and oak. Cloud forests have a high level of biodiversity, most of which is threatened due to unsustainable activities of humans.

## Your ribs move every time you breathe to the extent of about 5 million times a year

Humans have a set of 24 ribs, 12 on each side, which surround the chest and enable breathing. Ribs protect the heart and the lungs. The lungs inflate during breathing and the ribs move to accommodate the inflated lungs. This movement happens about five million times a year, corresponding to the number of times we breathe in a year.

## An electric eel can produce a shock of up to 650 volts

The electric eel is found in the rivers of South America, mostly the Amazon. It is actually a fish that does not have either a spine or teeth. It grows to about 2.5 m in length and its vital organs are located near its head. The rest of the body comprises muscles that generate electricity, and the nerve endings that discharge electricity. It uses small amounts of electricity to navigate through waters, to communicate and to stun small fish for feeding. However, it has the ability to discharge more than 600 volts of electricity, enough to create the sensation of shock on a human being.

## The e-mail is older than the World Wide Web

The e-mail predates the Internet or the World Wide Web by more than a decade. The e-mail originated in the research labs of the United States Defence Labs in the late 1960s, in the ARPANET project. It was used as a note or a file that was transferred from one user's folder to another user's folder in a mainframe computer. Several users could log in at a time to the mainframe computer from their respective 'dumb terminals' (computers that could not store data but could access the mainframe computer). Once any user logged in to a computer, he was able to see the message. However, it was not clear who sent the message and to whom. In 1971, Roy Tomlinson designated an e-mail address format, i.e., name of the user @ name of the computer, and used the 'at the rate of' @ symbol to separate the user from the host (computer). The Internet arrived on the scene some time in the early 1980s, almost ten years after the e-mail.

## The first vending machine was invented by Hero of Alexandria in the 1st century AD

Hero of Alexandria was a mathematician and an engineer about the time of Christ in the 1st century AD. He built a machine that could dispense holy water by accepting a coin. This was the world's first vending machine. Its internal structure comprised essentially of levers resembling a balance beam. On one end of the beam, a pan was attached. On the other end of the beam a plug was attached through a string, a plug that stopped the flow of water. When the coin was dropped inside the machine, it fell into the pan. The weight of the coin caused the lever to open a valve through which water trickled out. The pan continued to tilt due to the weight of the coin, and finally the coin fell off and the plug at the other end of the beam shut off the valve, and subsequently the flow of water.

## The world's densest wood, the black ironwood (*Olea laurifolia*) does not float on water and therefore sinks

The black ironwood is the wood from the tree *Olea laurifolia* found in the forests of the South Africa. It is the world's densest wood with a specific gravity of 1.49. It is also one of the heaviest woods with a weight of 452 kg per square metre. Owing to its specific gravity being higher than water, it sinks in water.

## The only known rock, which can float on water is pumice

Pumice is a volcanic rock, which is made from lava. It is a very light rock material filled with gas bubbles. It is produced when lava with a high gas and water content erupts from a volcano and then cools abruptly. During the process, the dissolved water vapours in the lava are suddenly released, resulting in the whole mass swelling up into a froth and solidifying due to abrupt cooling. Pumice is 90 per cent porous and lightweight and is the only kind of rock that can float on water.

## The word engineer comes from a Latin word meaning 'cleverness'

The root of the word engineer lies in the Latin word *ingenium*, meaning 'innate quality of mental power' or cleverness. In olden days, the engineers were required to be extremely skilful and inventive as they devised various levers, pulleys and other machines that helped in the civil and military development of any society. Engineer, as a verb, means to skillfully plan or manage a project or an enterprise.

## For each minute of the day, 1 billion tons of rain fall on the earth

Rain is a form of precipitation of water droplets that are greater than 0.5 mm in diameter. The amount of precipitation that falls around the world may range from less than 0.1 inch per year in some deserts to more than 900 inches per year in the tropics. It is estimated that every minute one billion tons (907 million tons) of water fall on the earth.

## No two snow flakes look the same

The structure of a snowflake is quite complex. It is formed from a frozen drop of cloud, which forms the nucleus. The nucleus quickly attracts water molecules around it that freeze instantly. In the process the attracted water molecules branch out giving the snowflake a unique hexagonal shape. Since the branching out process is different in each case, it is highly unlikely that two snowflakes would look the same.

## Of all known forms of animal life ever to inhabit the earth, only about 10 per cent exist today

The animal life on earth has seen at least five major mass extinctions in the millions of years of its existence. A noteworthy period of mass extinctions is the Permian-Triassic extinction event that occurred about 252 million years ago. The event saw the extinction of about 96 per cent of the marine life and 70 per cent of terrestrial life over a considerable period of time. It is estimated that the five mass extinction events in the 500 millions of years wiped out 90 per cent of the animal species from the face of the earth.

## Badminton originated from a sport in India called 'Poona'

Badminton is a popular game played with lightweight racquets and a shuttlecock. It is said to have been originated in Poona, now Pune, where the British army officers picked it up in the 1860s. The game was called Poona. It was introduced in England in about 1873 at the country estate of the Duke of Beaufort in Gloucestershire, England. The estate was called Badminton, after which the name Badminton was given to the sport.

## The cigarette lighter was invented before the matchbox

A cigarette lighter is a device used to generate a flame. It was invented sometime in the 16th century. The German chemist Johann Wolfgang Döbereiner in 1823 invented a kind of lighter that was called Döbereiner's lamp. But the first modern, self-igniting match was invented in 1805 by Jean Chancel. In London, matches meant for lighting cigars were introduced in 1849 by a shopkeeper named Heurtner.

## A piece of a neutron star of the size of a pin point would weigh 1 million tons

A neutron star is a remnant of a star after it has collapsed due to its own gravity. These stars are composed of subatomic particles called neutrons without any electrical charge. These stars could be two times the mass of the sun. The neutron stars have a very high surface gravity which could be $2 \times 10^{11}$ times more than the gravity on the surface of the earth. A neutron star is very dense. It is so dense that one teaspoon (5 millilitres) of its material would have a mass over $5.5 \times 10^{12}$ kg.

## Olympic gold medals are actually made mostly of silver

The Olympic gold medals are mostly made of silver, not gold. Only six grams, or 0.19 ounce, of gold is required to coat the medal. The medal itself is made of 92.5 per cent or 550 grams of pure silver. The medals are usually circular with a diameter of a minimum of 60 mm and a thickness of a minimum of 3 mm. These specifications are as per the Olympic Charter. The last time a pure gold medal was awarded was in the 1912 Olympics in Sweden.

## Some large asteroids even have their own moon

Asteroids are small rocky bodies that orbit the sun. Most asteroids orbit in a belt between Mars and Jupiter called the asteroid belt. They are sometimes called planetoids or minor planets. There are an estimated 400,000 asteroids. However, the large asteroids of about 100 km diameter are few. Some large asteroids have their own moon, such as the asteroid Ida, which has a tiny moon named Dactyl.

## The Great Pyramid of Giza is the result of an accumulation of 2.5 million blocks

The Great Pyramid of Giza is the oldest and the largest pyramid of Egypt. It was built for the Pharaoh Khufu (Cheops in Greek) and took 20 years to complete. The length of each side at the base averages 755.75 feet (230 metres). Its original height was 481.4 feet (147 metres), its present height is 455.4 feet (138.8 metres). It is made of about 2.5 million blocks of stone.

## Good Friday had once fallen on a Boxing Day

Boxing Day is a bank or public holiday that occurs on 26th December. On 26th December, 1899, a horse jump race was organized at Wolverhampton and a race horse fell down during the race. Its name was Good Friday.

## A crocodile always grows new teeth to replace the old teeth

The crocodile has 24 sharp teeth on each jaw, which are meant to grasp and crush, not to chew. The teeth are continuously replaced during the crocodile's lifetime. Each tooth is hollow and a new tooth grows inside the old one in order to be ready once the old tooth is lost. Young crocodiles can replace their teeth at a rate of one new tooth per socket each month.

## A rubber tyre is actually one single giant molecule

Rubber is a molecule that is found naturally in some plants (*Havea brasiliensis*) or can be manufactured synthetically from petroleum. The name rubber was coined by the English chemist Joseph Priestley in 1770 when he found it could be used to rub out pencil marks. The chemical structure of rubber comprises essentially of one type of molecule that is replicated several times (polymer) and connected together in the form of a chain.

## Douglas Engelbart, invented the first computer mouse in the year 1963 and it was made of wood

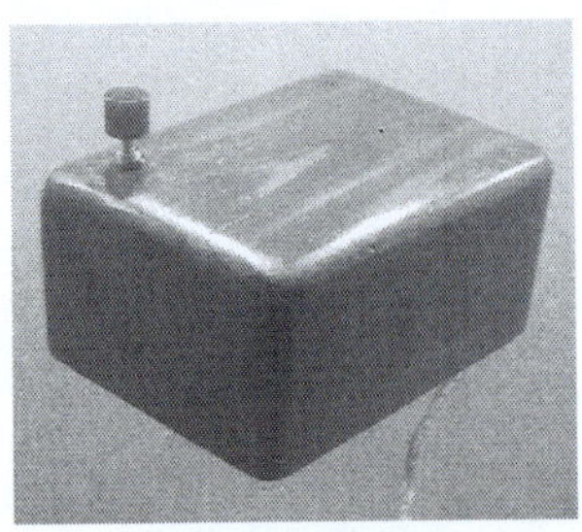

Douglas Carl Engelbart is an American inventor whose work mostly focused on human-computer interaction. He invented the computer mouse in the late 1960s. He received the patent in 1970. The mouse was made of a wooden shell with two wheels. He never received any royalties for his mouse invention.

## Jellyfish evaporates at times

Jellyfish are free swimming invertebrate animals found in the oceans. They are one of the oldest animals on earth dating from more than 500 million years ago. Most jellyfish are transparent and umbrella shaped. They are made of 98 per cent water. If a jellyfish washes up to the shore, it immediately evaporates and becomes almost invisible.

## The earth spins at the rate of 1,000 miles (1,600 km) per hour

The earth spins or rotates on its axis every day. It takes 24 hours to rotate once on its axis. To calculate the rate of rotation, the circumference of the earth at the equator, which is 25,000 miles, is divided by the total time taken per rotation, which is 24 hours. The value comes to be approximately 1,000 miles per hour or 1,600 km per hour, which is equivalent to covering the distance between Delhi and Mumbai in 52 minutes (approx.)—quite a high speed indeed.

## The Boeing 747–400 has six million parts

The Boeing 747–400 is one of the best selling Boeing 747 models. It was launched in 1985. The Boeing 747–400 is a complicated machine with six million parts. It is estimated that half of these parts are the fasteners, such as nuts, bolts, screws, etc. The parts are manufactured by different companies such as Northrop and Daewoo.

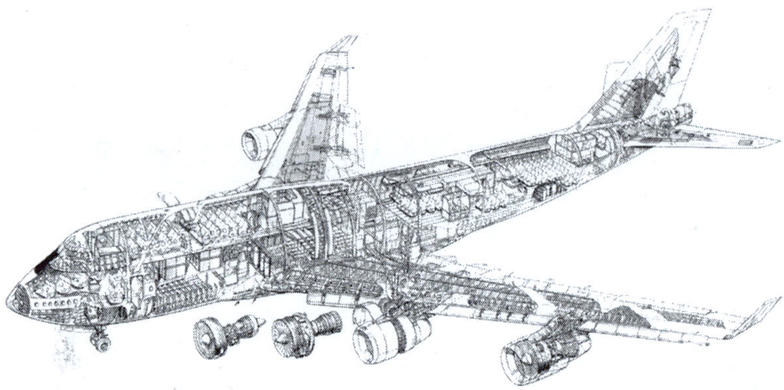

## Recycling 100 million mobile phones would recover 3.4 metric tons of gold

The average mobile phone contains about 24 mg of gold. Gold does not corrode, and therefore is a good transmitter of small amounts of currents in the mobile phone. It is estimated that in the United States alone, 130 million mobile phones are retired every year. Recycling these alone would yield about 3.4 metric tons of gold.

## The last date when every digit was odd was 19.11.1999. Next time it will be on 1.1.3111

The last totally odd numbered date any of us had seen in our lifetimes is 19.11.1999. It was the last calendar date composed of all odd digits that would occur for a very long time. The next odd day will be 1.1.3111, which is well over a thousand years away.

## Each king in a deck of playing cards represents a great king from history

A deck of cards has 52 cards of different denominations starting from one to ten and four colours, such as spades, clubs, hearts and diamonds. It has 4 types of court cards including King, Queen, and Jack. Interestingly, the Kings represent a real historical king. The king of Spades represents King David. The king of Clubs represents Alexander the Great. The king of Hearts represents Charlemagne and the king of Diamonds represents Julius Caesar.

## Pigeons can fly about 1,000 km a day

Pigeons have been domesticated since ancient times to carry messages. They used to travel several miles to deliver messages. Even today, pigeon posts exist that serve the military in many countries. Pigeons have also been domesticated for a sport called pigeon racing. The racing is timed and it has been found that the competing pigeons can fly up to 1,750 km a day.

## A jellyfish does not have a brain

The jellyfish has a network of nerves, just below the body surface, throughout its body. This network of nerves performs the functions of a brain. It senses the outside stimuli through these nerves and transmits the impulses to a circular nerve ring called the rhopalial lappet. This nerve ring is located on the circular periphery of the body of the jellyfish.

## Istanbul, Turkey is the only city in the world located on two continents

Istanbul is the capital of Turkey. It extends both on the European (Thrace) and on the Asian (Anatolia) sides of the Bosphorus Strait. Thus it is the only city in the world that is situated on two continents—Asia and Europe.

## Each time lightning strikes, some ozone gas is produced, thus strengthening the ozone layer in the earth's atmosphere

Ozone is a chemical compound made of three oxygen atoms. It is present in high amounts in the atmosphere as a layer known as the ozone layer between about 10 km and 50 km above the earth's surface. This layer is very precious for the sustenance of life on earth as it blocks the harmful ultraviolet rays of the sun that could destroy life. A small amount of ozone is formed when lightning strikes the earth's atmosphere. A lightning discharges ionizing radiation which results in the breakup of oxygen molecules into oxygen atoms. During this process, three such oxygen atoms quickly recombine to form the ozone molecule.

## Jupiter is larger than 1,000 earths

Jupiter is the fifth planet from the sun and the largest in our solar system. Jupiter is the third brightest thing in the night sky after moon and Venus. It is 317.83 times massive than the earth, and more than 1,000 earths could fit into it. Jupiter is essentially made of hydrogen and helium gases and liquid matter; it does not have a solid surface. The average distance between Jupiter and the Sun is 778 million km (about 5.2 times the average distance from the Earth to the Sun) and it completes an orbit every 11.86 earth years. It has about 66 moons, with four large moons called the Galilean moons—'Io', 'Europa', 'Ganymede' and 'Callisto'. Jupiter has been explored by the spacecrafts 'Voyager' and 'Pioneer' and other fly by spacecrafts. NASA plans to study Jupiter in detail using the spacecraft 'Juno', launched in August 2011, which will arrive at Jupiter in late 2016. The next planned mission to the Jovian system will be the European Space Agency's Jupiter Icy Moon Explorer (JUICE), due to launch in 2022.

## The birthday of Mahendra Singh Dhoni falls on 7$^{th}$ of July. Since the date is 7/7 he wears the jersey number 7

Mahendra Singh Dhoni is one of the successful captains of the Indian Cricket team. He is the recipient of the prestigious Padma Shri award. He was born on 7$^{th}$ July. He successfully captained *inter alia* at the win of the T20 World Cup in 2007, World Cup in 2011 by the Indian cricket team and the 4–0 brownwash of Australia in 2013, also at the win of the Chennai Super Kings at the two IPLs and one World T20 Championship. So he wears the jersey number 7 during all his matches.

## Alexander Graham Bell invented the first wireless telephone called 'photophone'

The photophone was a device that allowed for the transmission of sound on a beam of sunlight. It was invented jointly by Alexander Graham Bell and his assistant Charles Sumner Tainter. A mirror was allowed to vibrate under the action of a human voice. The mirror would become concave or convex and disperse or focus the light depending on the vibration. This light was picked up by the selenium cells in the receiver that gave the voice output. Bell considered the photophone to be his most important invention, which it indeed was as it transmitted the world's first wireless telephone message on April 1, 1880 between him and his assistant at a distance of 700 feet. The photophone is recognized as the progenitor of the modern fiber optics that today transmits over eighty per cent of the world's telecommunications.

## The word 'toy' comes from an old English word that means 'tool'

The English, before the 19th century, used the word 'toy' to mean 'tool'. It was meant to denote any object of little or no value, or fun value. It was definitely not used for describing a child's plaything. After the 19th century the word 'toy' became prominent to describe children's playthings.

## Dipsomania refers to an insatiable craving for alcoholic beverages

The term dipsomania is derived from two Greek words that mean *dipso* (thirst) and *mania* (abnormal mood). The term was coined by the German physician C.W. Hufeland in 1819 to indicate an abnormal thirst, chiefly for alcohol. The medical condition of dipsomaniacs is considered to be acute state of habitual drunkenness.

## Neptune was the first planet in our solar system to be discovered mathematically

Neptune is the eighth planet from the sun in our solar system. The discovery of Neptune was made when the astronomers observed that the seventh planet from the sun, Uranus, did not orbit in the way it was supposed to. Looking at this irregularity, the French mathematician Urbain Joseph Le Verrier predicted the presence of another planet. Le Verrier also predicted the mass and position of this planet accurately. Following Le Verrier's mathematical calculations, Johann Gottfried Galle in Berlin discovered Neptune in 1846.

## The brain does not feel pain

The human body has pain receptors or sensory neurons (a type of cell) in all its parts. The job of these receptors is to pass on stimuli to the brain, which provides us the awareness of pain. However, the brain does not contain any sensory receptors and so when it gets a stimuli, it is not able to feel the pain as our arms or legs do.

## Sanskrit is considered as the mother of all higher languages. It has the most precise grammar, and therefore a suitable language for computer software

Researchers have discovered that Sanskrit, which was spoken thousands of years ago in India, and which is still spoken, is the most unambiguous and perfect language in the world. Its precise grammar is extremely useful to develop computer software because the computer is able to process the precise sentences in Sanskrit.

## Every drop of seawater contains approximately 1 billion gold atoms

The total quantity of gold dissolved in seawater is estimated to be 13.7 million tons. That means one drop of seawater contains 1 billion gold atoms. Considering the high economic value of gold, many people in the past have tried to recover gold from the sea, but without any success. The most notable of them was Fritz Haber, the German inventor. Till date gold has not been successfully extracted commercially from seawater.

## Karaoke in Japanese means 'empty orchestra'

Karaoke is a kind of music that plays the song minus the vocal. The music could be a popular tune or song. Since only the orchestra is played and the vocal is missing, it is called the 'empty orchestra'. A participant can sing along with the music using a microphone.

## The first microphone was invented by Emile Berliner in 1876

In 1876 Emile Berliner saw the working of a Bell Company telephone being demonstrated at an exhibition, and later, on exploring the transmitter, immediately decided that it could be suitably modified. He came up with the idea of a microphone inside the telephone that could transmit speech with an increased volume.

## The burning sensation we get from chilli peppers is because of a chemical called capsaicin

Capsaicin is a chemical compound found in chillies. It is present in the tissue, which supports the seeds in the chillies. The natural function of capsaicin is to protect the seeds from animals and fungi. When eaten, capsaicin produces a biting and burning sensation on the tongue. It can produce burning sensation on the skin as well. It is used in food to add heat to the food. The degree of heat is measured on the Scoville scale. The number of Scoville Heat Units (SHU) indicates the amount of capsaicin present in the food. The bell pepper has zero SHU whereas the Naga chilli has an SHU of 2,00,000.

## The surface area of the human lung is almost equivalent to one side of a tennis court

The human lung is the chief organ that facilitates respiration and exchange of gases. There are two lungs that contain a total of about 300 million to 500 million alveoli. These alveoli have a total surface area of about 70 square metres, which is approximately the size of one side of a singles tennis court.

## Sir Arthur Conan Doyle, the creator of Sherlock Holmes, was an avid cricketer

Sir Arthur Conan Doyle is the well known creator of the fictitious detective Sherlock Holmes. However, it is not that well known that Sir Doyle also loved to play cricket. In fact he named Sherlock after amalgamating the names of two Nottinghamshire cricketers, Mordecai Sherwin and Frank Shacklock. Sir Doyle was, in fact, part of the first team to tour the Netherlands in 1891. He only took one wicket in his career but it was memorable – dismissing W.G. Grace for 110.

## Salt is the only rock humans can eat

Salt is a crystalline mineral, which is obtained from the sea or rocks. Sea salt is usually composed of sodium and chlorine, with extremely small amounts of other elements, such as calcium and magnesium. The table salt that we eat is mostly sodium chloride. Salt is essential for humans because the sodium contained in it acts as a messenger and helps the transfer of nerve impulses, or electrical signals from one part of the body to another.

## The word Karate means, 'empty hand'

Karate is a Japanese word derived from *Kara* meaning 'empty' and *te* meaning 'hand'. Karate is a style of martial art that involves combating empty handed, without using any form of armament. In this type of combat, any suitable part of the body is used, such as palms, elbows, knees, heels, etc.

## The typical lifetime of a small cumulus cloud is between 10 to 15 minutes

Cumulus cloud is a type of cloud that looks like cotton. They form as the ground heats up during the day. They are found at heights ranging from 600 metres above ground in winter to about 1,000 metres in summer. The small cumulus clouds are often short lived with an average lifetime of 15 minutes.

## A bee sting is acidic and a wasp sting is alkaline

Bees and wasps have a strong organ that is used to inject poison or venom into the body of an animal or human. The venom of a bee is essentially a protein, called apitoxin, and is acidic in nature. The venom of a wasp is also a protein but it is alkaline in nature. Pompilidotoxin is an example of wasp venom. To treat a sting by one of these one should use the opposite type of chemical. When one is stung by a bee, one should wash the injury area with an alkaline substance such as bicarbonate of soda to neutralize the acid, thereby reducing the pain. When one is stung by a wasp, one should wash the area with an acid such as vinegar to neutralize the alkali.

## The tank containing all the rocket fuel weighs seven times more than the space shuttle itself

A rocket needs fuel to launch itself. The fuel or propellant is a chemical that could be either liquid or solid. When it burns, it produces a high volume of gas, which is ejected backwards at very high speed, thus providing a forward thrust to the vehicle. There are engines at the back of the shuttle but no place for fuel. The fuel is carried externally in a tank. About 90 per cent of the weight of a typical rocket is due to the amount of the fuel it carries.

## Abraham Lincoln and Charles Darwin were born on the same day

Abraham Lincoln was the sixteenth President of the United States of America. His leadership in ending the Civil War and abolishing slavery changed the history of America forever. Charles Darwin was a British naturalist whose work on 'The Origin of Species' was one of the monumental works of science that forever changed the way we look at creation and evolution, and this is very well acknowledged. Both these personalities were born on the same day, i.e., 12.2.1809.

## The bank credit card called 'MasterCard' was known as 'Master Charge'

In 1966, several banks in California merged to bring out a credit card. This card was called Master Charge: The Inter Bank Card. This was renamed in 1980 to what is now known as MasterCard.

## India's first airmail flight took off from Allahabad for Naini on 18th February 1911

India's first airmail flight took off carrying 6,500 letters on 18th February 1911. The pilot of the two-seater aeroplane was a Frenchman Henry Pequet who flew 10 km across the Yamuna from Allahabad to Naini in about 13 minutes.

## The colour of the black box in an aeroplane is orange

The black box is an equipment in an aeroplane, which contains the cockpit voice recorder and the flight data recorder. The black box helps investigators to determine the cause of an airplane crash. The black box was invented by an Australian scientist David Warren. The boxes are painted bright orange so that they can be located easily after a crash.

## A snail has about 25,000 teeth

Snails are soft bodied animals (mollusks) that have an outer shell when they become adults. Snails are found in land, fresh water and sea water. The snails have radula, a ribbon like structure in the mouths, which have rows of several thousand teeth arranged on it, just like a saw. The snails use them for filtering small algae and other extremely small animals (planktons). Some carnivorous snails use the radula to tear the flesh of their prey.

## George Washington's false teeth were carved from hippopotamus ivory and cow's teeth and fixed together with metal springs

George Washington suffered from deteriorating teeth. By the time he was 22 years of age, all his teeth were extracted. Finally, he had to be given a set of dentures. The dentists devised the dentures using a variety of things, including ivory, gold, human and cow's teeth. These sets of teeth were held together with metal springs. He had many such dentures. With this cumbersome apparatus in his mouth, throughout his life, he had problems chewing food, speaking and smiling.

## Liquid air looks like water with a bluish tint

Liquid air is formed when air is compressed at very high pressure and simultaneously cooled to very low temperatures of below minus 150 degree celsius. Liquid air predominantly contains oxygen and nitrogen. The colour of liquid air is pale blue. Liquid air is used in several industries where the air is fractionated into oxygen and nitrogen, and the oxygen is used for welding, etc.

## The dollar symbol ($) is a U combined with an S (U.S.)

The dollar sign $ is a monogram used on the money bags issued by the United States mint. The 'U' and 'S' are superimposed on each other where the bottom part of the 'U' merges with that of 'S'. The origin of the sign is believed to be from the Spanish peso, which was written as $p^s$.

## A chameleon's tongue is twice the length of its body

A chameleon is a kind of lizard that eats small insects. It uses its unique tongue to catch its prey. The tongue is coiled inside its mouth. During preying, the tongue projects out with a force, which the scientists call the ballistic mechanism, to capture the prey. The tongue can project up to the double the size of the chameleon's body. Sometimes the tongue may extend up to 600 per cent of its original resting size.

## The heart of a shrimp is located in its head

Shrimp is a kind of crustacean that occurs in all oceans, freshwater lakes and streams. Shrimps range in length from a few millimetres to more than 20 centimetres (about 8 inches). They are an important source of food for humans. The body of the shrimp has two main parts—the abdomen and the cephalothorax (head and thorax fused together). The cephalothorax is covered with a carapace. The heart is located in the cephalothorax.

## Dimples on a golf ball help reduce drag, allowing the ball to fly further than a ball without dimples

Dimples are the indentations that are made on the surface of a golf ball. The golf balls were made of *gutta percha,* a packing material, and the players discovered that the scratches and nicks helped the ball to fly more favourably. The gutta was therefore hammered at regular intervals to increase the consistency of the ball's play. Soon afterwards, the Balata ball was discovered, which essentially wrapped a rubber sheath on a rubber core of the ball. The manufacturers used a mold to produce dimples on to the surface. A typical dimple on a golf ball is 2-5 mm in diameter and about 0.2 mm deep. Modern golf balls have 300-450 dimples of varying sizes.

## Honey does not spoil

Honey is made by the honey bees from the nectar of flowers. Honey is composed mainly of sugar. It gets its sweetness from glucose and fructose. It also contains granulated sugar. Honey is viscous and contains very little water (about 16 per cent). This prevents the micro organisms, such as bacteria and fungal spores from growing in honey. Honey, therefore, does not spoil easily.

## 40 tons of space dust falls on the earth every day

Space scientists estimate that daily about 40 tons of cosmic or space dust falls on earth. They are studying this dust by collecting them using high altitude aircrafts and satellites. The origin of this dust is not clear, however, it is speculated that in space the asteroids, meteors and comets collide, thus producing dust.

## Ostriches yawn in groups before they go to sleep

It is known that all vertebrate animals yawn. The cause of yawning is not fully understood, but it is surely contagious. Ostriches are known to yawn as soon as they are hatched. Yawning happens mostly before sleep. At night, when ostriches are ready to settle down, they yawn in groups. First, the leader yawns, followed by the rest of the group. This is the way the leader communicates to the flock to all settle down.

## Linus Pauling is the only person who has been awarded two unshared Nobel Prizes

Linus Pauling was a chemist who contributed immensely to the knowledge of chemistry and biological molecules. For his research of the chemical bonds and their application to find out the structure of complex molecules, he was awarded the Nobel Prize in Chemistry in 1954. Since 1946, Pauling had ceaselessly championed against the nuclear tests and all forms of war, which was used as a means to solve national and international conflicts, for which he was awarded the Nobel Peace Prize in 1962.

## The longest suspension bridge in the world is the Akashi Kaikyō Bridge in Kobe, Japan. It has an amazing central span of 1991 metres (6,532 feet)

The Akashi Kaikyō bridge links the island of Honshu to Awaji island. It has a central span length of 1991 metres, the longest span of any bridge on earth. There are other two spans or sections, each measuring 960 metres or 3,150 feet. The bridge has a total length of 3,911 metres or 12,831 feet. It has six lanes and 23,000 cars pass through it each day. It is also called the Pearl bridge.

## Pure alkali metals, such as sodium, potassium, are stored in kerosene to prevent explosion

Alkali metals are chemical elements that are highly reactive with oxygen in the air and water. The alkali metals are sodium, potassium, rubidium, cesium, and francium. When any of these metals are dropped in water, an explosion takes place with the generation of heat. The alkali metal breaks water into its constituents, hydrogen and hydroxyl ions, and due to the heat, the hydrogen gas catches fire. They react immediately with oxygen in air to form oxides, and hence pure alkali metals are not found in nature. Due to their highly reactive nature, pure alkali metals are stored in kerosene or mineral oil (paraffin).

## A lightning bolt travels at about 14,000 miles per hour (2,20,000 km) and brings 3,00,000 volts of electricity to the ground

A lightning is usually produced by the cumulonimbus clouds in the atmosphere. In the clouds, negative and positive electric fields are formed from top to bottom containing negative and positive ions, respectively. A column of ions (leader bolt) moves from the negatively charged part to the positively charged part, discharging electricity. The speed of such a bolt could exceed 2,20,000 kilometres per hour, that is 14,000 miles per hour, and can reach a temperature of more than 30,000 degree celsius.

## The time taken by glass to decompose is one million years

Glass is a solid, transparent material made chiefly of silica. Other elements, such as sodium and calcium are also added. According to an estimate by the United States Environmental Protection Agency, about 13 million tons of glass waste is generated annually in the US. The decomposition of glass depends on a lot of factors, such as temperature, oxygen levels and the presence of water. Most of the time, the glass is recycled into new items.

## The whale shark has over 4,000 teeth

Whales are the largest known animals of the earth. They typically measure more than 60 feet; with the blue whale measuring about 98 feet. Not all whales have teeth. Only the toothed whale has in its mouth several rows of tiny teeth that resemble a rasp (a kind of flat tool with sharp projections to work on wood).

## A cow gives nearly 2,00,000 glasses of milk in its lifetime

A cow produces large amount of milk in its lifetime. An average cow of a good breed produces about 13 to 15 litres of milk per day. That translates to about 90 glasses (of 150 ml capacity) of milk per day or 16,000 glasses of milk per year. A cow on an average produces milk for about 12 years.

## Dr. Bidhan Chandra Roy, the architect of modern Bengal was born on 1st July 1882 and died on 1st July 1962

Dr. Bidhan Chandra Roy was a doctor and a freedom fighter who went on to become the second chief minister of West Bengal in 1948 at Gandhiji's behest. Dr. Bidhan Chandra Roy was a philanthropist and took major interest in the social, cultural and industrial development of West Bengal. He was awarded Bharat Ratna for his exemplary service in 1961. He died when he was exactly 80 years old, on the same day he was born, i.e., 1st July.

## Only one satellite has been destroyed by a meteor, and it was the European Space Agency's Olympus-1 in 1993

Olympus-1 was a communications satellite, which was launched by the European Space Agency in 1989. In 1993, Olympus-1 was hit by a meteoroid that damaged its solar array pointing system. Satellites use panels of solar cells to derive electricity from the sun. For this, the solar panels have to point at the direction of the sun. A solar array pointing system is used to suitably point to solar arrays towards the sun. This pointing system was damaged.

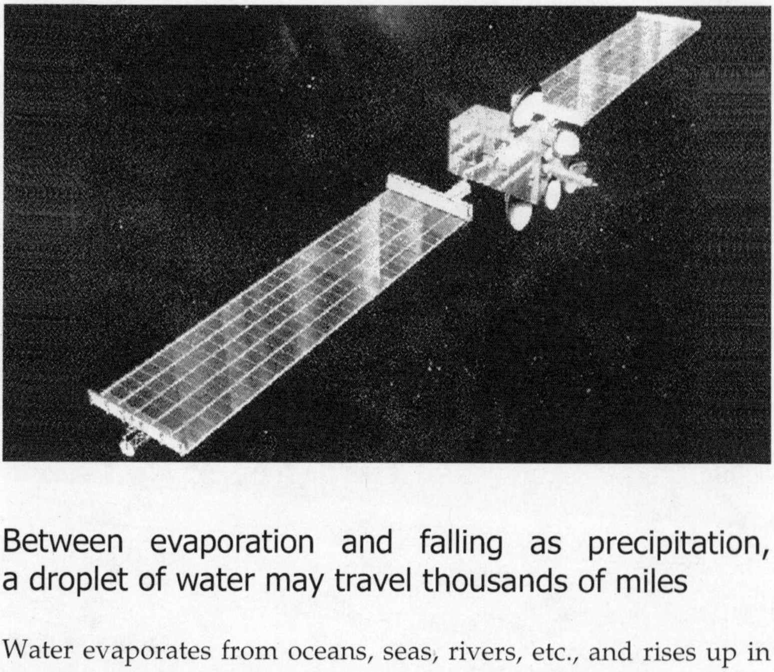

## Between evaporation and falling as precipitation, a droplet of water may travel thousands of miles

Water evaporates from oceans, seas, rivers, etc., and rises up in the atmosphere. At the height of several thousand kilometres, these vapours condense to form clouds and eventually droplets. By this time, the droplet may have travelled many miles from its place of origin. Once the droplets reach a certain size, typically 6 mm in diameter, they begin to fall from a great height and would travel nearly thousands of miles.

## The Calculus was discovered simultaneously by Isaac Newton and Gottfried Wilhelm Leibnitz

Calculus is a branch of mathematics, which studies 'change'. Accordingly, it deals with limits, derivatives, functions and indefinite series that explain 'change'. Isaac Newton and Gottfried Wilhelm Leibnitz independently invented calculus. Newton used calculus fundamentally to arrive at the universal law of gravitation and then to solve the problem of planetary motion, the shape of the surface of a rotating fluid, the oblateness of the earth, the motion of a weight sliding on a cycloid and also to explain various other interesting phenomenon. Leibnitz provided a clear set of rules for manipulating infinitesimal quantities, allowing the computation of second and higher derivatives, and providing the product rule and chain rule, in their differential and integral forms.

## For every triangle there is a Nine Point Circle

The three mid points (D, E, F) of the three sides, BC, CA, AB; the three feet of the altitudes (G, H, I); and the midpoint of the line segment from each vertex of the triangle (J, K, L) to the orthocentre (S, where the three altitudes meet) are concyclic. The corresponding circle is called the Nine Point Circle.

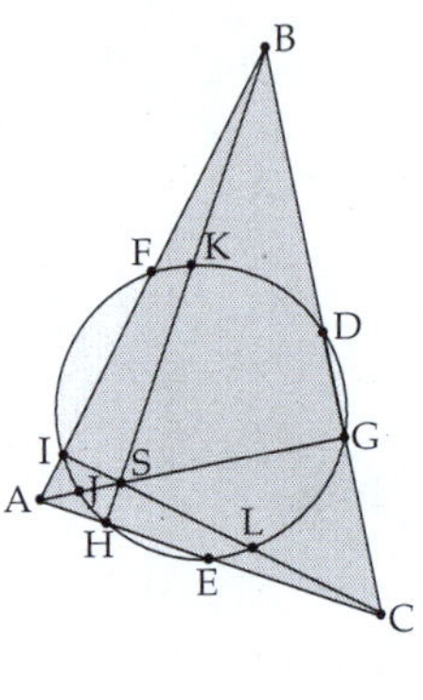

## Simson's line exhibits a peculiar collinearity

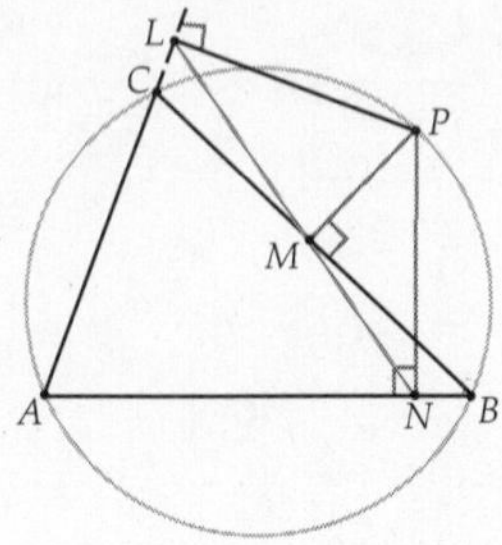


The feet of the perpendiculars (L, M, N) drawn from a point 'P' on the circumcircle of a triangle ABC are always collinear. This line, LMN, is called Simson's line, after Robert Simson (1687–1786), a Scottish mathematician, who first identified this line.

## The Möbius Strip was discovered simultaneously by August Ferdinand Möbius and Johann Benedict Listing

The Möbius strip is formed by taking a rectangular strip of paper and connecting its ends after giving it a half twist. It is a surface with only one side and one edge. See lemniscate at page 8. The properties of the strip were discovered independently and almost simultaneously by two German mathematicians, August Ferdinand Möbius and Johann Benedict Listing, in 1858.

## Fermat's last theorem

The relation $a^n + b^n = c^n$, for $a, b, c, n$ being integers is valid for $n$ being limited to 1 and 2. For example

$$3^1 + 4^1 = 7^1$$
$$24^2 + 7^2 = 25^2$$

Fermat's last theorem was first stated by Pierre de Fermat, a 17th century lawyer and amateur mathematician. The proposition states that the equation, $a^n + b^n = c^n$, where $a$, $b$ and $c$ are non-zero integers, has no solutions for $n > 2$.

## The Theory of Evolution was discovered simultaneously by Charles Darwin and Alfred Russel Wallace

The theory of evolution states that species evolved as a result of natural selection, and that species could adapt in harsh conditions. This theory was put forth simultaneously by the two English naturalists Charles Darwin and Alfred Russel Wallace.

## Wireless transmission was discovered simultaneously by J.C. Bose and Marconi

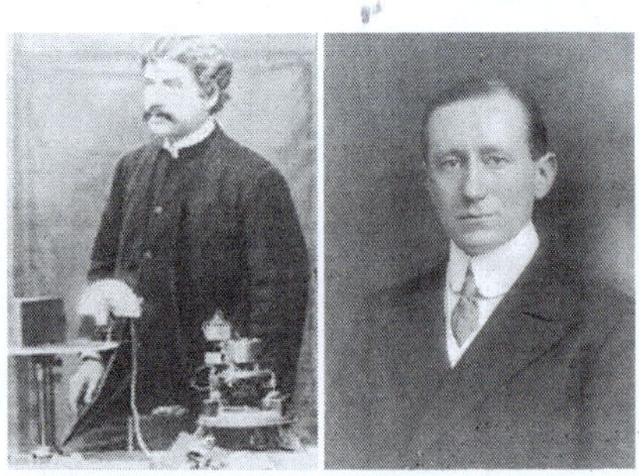

Professor Jagadish Chandra Bose demonstrated that the electric rays had the ability to travel long distances without the help of any wire. He did so by initiating the electric rays using a radiator in the lecture room, which passed through three solid walls of the lecture room, an intervening room, to a third room. The receiver of the radiation used the incoming rays to ring a bell, discharge a pistol, and explode a miniature mine. Bose never patented his findings. Almost about the same time, Guglielmo Marconi devised a system using transmitter, coherers and receivers that could send wireless signals through long distances. He was successful in patenting the system and commercializing it.

## Kronecker's delta is a function of integers

Kronecker's delta is defined as

$$\delta_{ij} = \begin{cases} 0, & \text{if } i \neq j \\ 1, & \text{if } i = j \end{cases}$$

For example, $\delta_{12} = 0$, whereas $\delta_{33} = 1$.

Kronecker's delta is a function between two variables, which are integers. The function is 1 if the two variables are the same or equal, and the function is zero if the two variables are not the same or unequal. This function is named after Leopold Kronecker, a German mathematician, who discovered it. He once said 'The integers came from God and all else was man-made'.

## The only example of $x^m - y^n = 1$, when $x, y, m, n$ are integers is $3^2 - 2^3 = 1$

The unique example is of the form,

$$x^y - y^x = 1$$

with $y = m = 2$

and $x = n = 3$

$$x^m - y^n = 1$$

Here

$x = 3$

$y = 2$

$m = 2$

$n = 3$

## Primates appear to have some sense of numbers

Michael Beran, a scientist at the Georgia State University trained chimps to use a computer and a joystick. The computer screen showed a numeral, followed by a series of dots. The chimps had to match the numeral with the dots. One chimp learned numerals from 1 to 7, while another managed to learn till the numeral 6.

## A Saharan ant travels long distances to trace its food, but does not return the same way like other ants. It rather comes through a different route

*Cataglyphis fortis*, a Saharan desert ant travels long distances over sandy terrain, often completely devoid of landmarks, as it searches for food. They are able to return to their nest not by retracing their outbound path, but by using a direct route. They use light from the sky, but it seems they have a built-in pedometer that counts their steps and allows them to measure exact distances. An ant may travel 50 metres to catch an insect, tear a piece of the insect and carry it back to the nest through a hole often less than a millimetre in diameter.

## Earth and Venus are often called twins

Venus is only 40 million kilometres closer to the sun than we are. Its size is very much like the earth. But this small distance of 40 million kilometres has made all the difference. Venus and Earth are often called twins because of their similar size, mass, density, composition and gravity. However, Venus is the hottest planet in the solar system with its surface temperature reaching about 465 degrees celsius.

## The world's bestsellers were named differently

The bestselling books by eminent authors were named differently. The book *Gone with the Wind* by Margaret Mitchell was named *Ba Ba Black Sheep*; *War and Peace* by Leo Tolstoy was named *All's Well that Ends Well*; and *Frankenstein* by Mary Shelly was named *Prometheus Unchained*.

## $2\pi(R + 1) - 2\pi R = 6.28$ (approx.) irrespective of the value of $R$. What does it imply?

According to this formula, where $R$ is the radius of earth, if you encircle the earth with a band that is placed one metre away from and above the equator the value would come to be 6.28 m. It means that if such a band is made to go round the earth over the equator, its length would be 6.28 m more than the equatorial circumference of the earth! Interestingly, if you encircle a small ball with a band placed one metre away from its diameter the value of the difference of the circumferences would still be 6.28 m.

## Dennis Overbye and his take on the laws of thermodynamics

Dennis Overbye is a science correspondent for the New York Times. He presented a humorous summary of the three principal laws of thermodynamics in his book *Lonely Hearts of the Cosmos: The Scientific Quest for the Secret of the Universe* published in 1991. The crux of the three laws of thermodynamics are simply stated as follows:

1. Whenever heat energy is converted into any other form of energy or vice versa, each is equivalent to the other. One cannot obtain energy without expending equivalent amount of energy of other form.
2. No engine working in a cycle is capable of converting the entire energy input in the form of heat to useful work.
3. Absolute zero is unattainable.

In his book, Dennis Overbye stated the above laws as follows:

1. You can't win
2. You can't break even
3. You can't go out of the game.

## Some interesting facts about the number 12

On December 12, 2012, the numbers of the day, month and year all matched, i.e., it was 12.12.12. The next such date will come on 1.1.2101. We present some other interesting facts about the number 12.

- 12 can be easily divided into halves, thirds, fourths, sixths and twelfths.
- 12 is commonly used in measurements. There are 12 inches in a foot, 12 ounces in a troy pound (used to measure gold, silver and gems), and 12 in a dozen.
- 12 often represents the end of one cycle and the beginning of another. December is the $12^{th}$ month of the year; every 12 hours day turns to night or night to day.
- There are 12 pairs of ribs in humans, 12 face cards in a deck, and 12 people have walked on the moon.

## To travel from earth to Sirius will take 18 hours if you travel at the speed of light

If you wish to travel from earth to the nearest star Sirius at 99.99999999% of the speed of light, it will take you 18 hours to reach Sirius. However, when you return to earth after another 18 hours with an intention of dinner, you will find that your family and friends would have already had 6,570 dinners. The explanation lies in the concept of time dilation of the special theory of relativity.

## Light does not age

Light is electromagnetic radiation. It travels at a very high speed. Time has no effect on it as it travels at a very high speed and so it does not age.

## John Kennedy and Aldous Huxley died on the same day

John Fitzgerald Kennedy was the $35^{th}$ President of the United States of America. At 43, he was one of the youngest Presidents of the USA. He is the only US President to have won the prestigious Pulitzer Prize. The notable events during his tenure were the Cuban missile crisis, building of Berlin War and the beginning of the Vietnam War. Aldous Leonard Huxley was an eminent English writer, who was also a humanist, pacifist and a satirist. He moved to Los Angeles and settled there. Some of his works are *Point Counter Point, Do What You Will, The Devils of Loudun and Island*. He also wrote an essay in a very poignant style on the 'Bose Institute', the research institution created by Sir J.C. Bose. Both Kennedy and Huxley died on the same day, i.e., November $22^{nd}$, 1963.

## Orville Wright and Mahatma Gandhi died on the same day

Orville Wright is considered the father of modern aviation. Together with his brother Wilbur, he invented the first airplane. He developed flight technology for the United States Army. Mahatma Gandhi, an international figure symbolizing peace, the Father of the Indian Nation, ushered in the Indian independence through non-violent means. Both Orville Wright and Mahatma Gandhi died on the same day, i.e., January $30^{th}$, 1948.

## Space-time curvature is a geometric property of the four dimensional space-time

Space and time are woven together to form a fourth dimension called space-time. Curvature is a geometric property of space-time. Einstein identified this property while he was working on his General Relativity theory. The curvature of space-time is directly related to the energy and the momentum of any matter or radiation. A standard way to illustrate this idea is to place a bowling ball (representing a massive object such as the sun) onto a stretched rubber sheet (representing space-time). If a marble is placed onto the rubber sheet, it will roll towards the bowling ball, and may even be put into 'orbit' around the bowling ball. This occurs, not because the smaller mass is 'attracted' by a force emanating from the larger one, but because it is travelling along a surface which has been deformed by the presence of the larger mass. In the same way gravitation in Einstein's theory arises not as a force propagating *through* space-time, but rather as a feature *of* space-time itself. According to Einstein, your weight on earth is due to the fact that your body is travelling through warped space-time!

## Moseley, Sukumar Ray, Schrödinger, Jamini Roy, and Srinivasa Ramanujan, all great innovators, were born in 1887

The year 2012 celebrated the 125 years of five innovators, Henry Moseley, Sukumar Ray, Erwin Schrödinger, Jamini Roy, and Srinivasa Ramanujan. Henry Gwyn Jeffreys Moseley was an English physicist who provided the explanation of X-ray spectra, which justified many concepts in chemistry by sorting the chemical elements of the Periodic Table of the Elements in a quite logical order based on their physics. He died at the age of 26 only at the First World War. Sukumar Ray was an Indian writer who was known for his humorous creations. He wrote poems, stories, and playrights exclusively for children. His innovative creations are sometimes called 'literary nonsense', but these were full of sense. He also died young at the age of 33, but before that he fathered Satyajit Ray, who later become a world famous film director. Erwin Rudolf Josef Alexander Schrödinger was an Austrian theoretical physicist who achieved fame for his contributions to quantum mechanics, especially the Schrödinger equation, for which he received the Nobel Prize in 1933. Jamini Roy was an Indian painter who experimented with tribal folk art and transformed them into innovative paintings with his new style of painting. Srinivasa Ramanujan Iyengar was an Indian mathematician and self taught genius who, with almost no formal training in pure mathematics, made substantial contributions to mathematical analysis, number theory, infinite series and continued fractions.

## Bizzare coincidences between the lives of Lincoln and Kennedy

The two famous Presidents of the United States of America, Abraham Lincoln and John F. Kennedy shared strange coincidences.

1. Abraham Lincoln was elected to Congress in 1846. John F. Kennedy was elected to Congress in 1946.
2. Abraham Lincoln was elected President in 1860. John F. Kennedy was elected President in 1960.
3. The names Lincoln and Kennedy, each contains seven letters.
4. Both were particularly concerned with Civil Rights.
5. Wives of both lost a child while living in the White House.
6. Both Presidents were shot on a Friday.
7. Both Presidents were shot in the head.
8. Both were accompanied by their wives when they were assassinated.
9. Both were assassinated by Southerners.
10. Both were cautioned before their assassination but none changed their engagements.
11. Lincoln was shot at the theatre named 'Kennedy.' Kennedy was shot in a car called a 'Lincoln.'
12. Both were succeeded by Southerners named Johnson.
13. Andrew Johnson, who succeeded Lincoln, was born in 1808. Lyndon Johnson, who succeeded Kennedy, was born in 1908. Both their names had thirteen letters.
14. Both assassins were known by their three names, John Wilkes Booth and Lee Harvey Oswald. Both names are composed of fifteen letters.

## The sum of the three angles of a spherical triangle is always greater than 180°

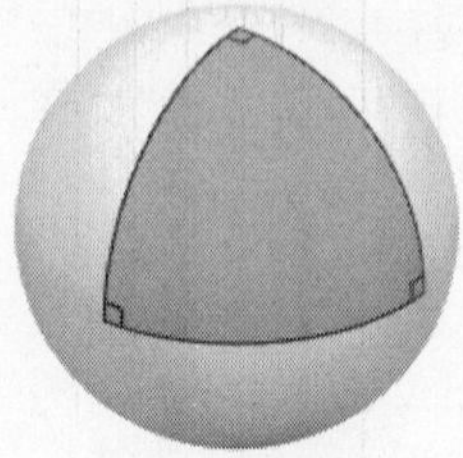

A spherical triangle is formed on the surface of a sphere by three arcs. When the magnitudes of the three angles are added, they have a value that is greater than 180°, which is the value for the sum of three angles of a normal triangle.

## Triskaidekaphobia is the fear of the number thirteen

Triskaidekaphobia is a word that arises from the greek *tris* meaning three and *deka* meaning ten, i.e., thirteen, and *phobia* meaning fear. Triskaidekaphobia, thus means the fear of the number thirteen. In western culture, the number thirteen is often associated with ill luck. Many hotels in the western countries have no thirteenth floor and many streets are avoided being given the number thirteen.

## Stefan Edberg and John McEnroe were born on the days when two famous political leaders rose to power

Stefan Edberg, the former World No. 1 tennis player was born on the same day as Indira Gandhi became India's Prime Minister, i.e., January 19, 1966. On January 19, 1966, the congress voted for its Prime Minister and Indira Gandhi received 355 votes, making her victorious. She held the office of prime minister with effect from January 24, 1966. John McEnroe, another World Champion in tennis was born on the same day when Fidel Castro seized power in Cuba, i.e., February 16, 1959.

## QWERTY keyboard sequence is about 129 years old

The QWERTY keyboard derives its name from the sequence of letters in the first row of the keyboard. It was invented by the American Christopher Latham Sholes in 1868, who had built the first typewriter and included this sequence of letters in the keyboard.

## Goldfish kept in dark room eventually turns white

Goldfish (*Carassius auratus auratus*) belong to the carp family to which the common carp or *Koi* fish belongs. They were originally domesticated as normal gray or silver fish by the ancient Chinese. In several cases, the grey fish produced mutated fish that were yellow, orange or red. The yellowish orange (golden) fish were chosen to be further domesticated by the Chinese. Today goldfish is kept in aquariums at homes throughout the world. When goldfish is kept in a dark room for many days, it turns white.

## If you leave Tokyo by plane at 7:00 am, you will arrive in Honolulu at approximately 4:30 pm the previous day

There is a massive gap in time zones between Honolulu and Tokyo. Honolulu is 19 hours behind Tokyo. Subtracting the 7 hours and 45 minutes flight time between these two cities gives us a trip difference of 11 hours and 15 minutes. Therefore, you would actually reach Honolulu more than 11 hours before you left Japan.

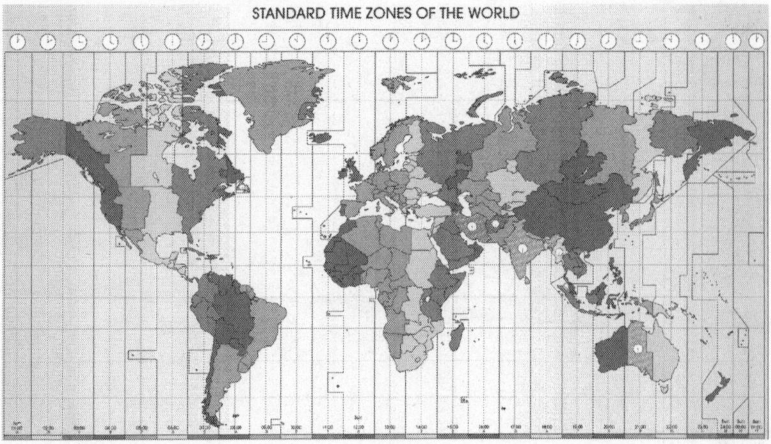


## There can be a month without full moon

There are usually twelve full moons in a year, usually once a month. This is because of the waxing and waning of the moon. It takes about 29 days for the moon to complete its cycle and return to its starting phase. So in months that have less than 29 days, which is only February, this phenomenon could happen. And it happens more frequently than you think. There was no Full Moon in February for the years 1809, 1847, 1866, 1885, 1915, 1934, 1961, and as recently as 1999.

## Dolphins sleep with one eye open

Dolphins are mammals that are found in the seas and oceans. When the dolphins sleep, they seem to float on water with one eye open. This is because they sleep with one part of the brain at a time. The other half is awake and that keeps one eye open. If they sleep and become unconscious, they would suffocate or drown. To prevent this, they sleep with half of their brain. After some time they close the eye and open the other eye and sleep.

## The golden eagles can spot a rabbit from nearly 3 km away

The golden eagle (*Aquila chrysaetos*) is one of the largest birds of prey, a predator bird. It is mostly found in America and Mexico. They are very swift, and can dive upon their prey at speeds of more than 241 km per hour. All eagles have very sharp eyesight—four to five times stronger than a human with perfect vision. They can spot movement long distances away. An eagle can easily see a rabbit on the ground from 3 km away.

## Waste produced by one chicken in its lifetime could supply enough electricity to run a 100 W bulb for 5 hours

It is estimated that a 1.8 kg chicken will produce 28 to 100 grams of manure per day or 12 to 36 kg of manure per year. In its lifetime, a chicken can produce enough manure to power a 100 watt lightbulb for 5 hours. The manure produced by chicken can be decomposed to produce methane, which in turn can drive turbines to produce electricity. In fact in Britain, Mr. Harold Bate has invented a car that runs on methane produced from chicken manure.

## In Garhwal there are five places each for the worship of Vishnu (Panch Badri), and Shiva (Panch Kedar), and five places where two holy rivers unite (Panch Prayag)

Garhwal is known as a part of Dev Bhumi, meaning the land of God. It has many holy places and rivers. It has five places for the worship of Vishnu, called Panch Badri. These are: Vishal Badri (Badrinath), Yogadhyan Badri, Bhavishya Badri, Vriddha Badri and Adi Badri. Garhwal also has five places for worshipping Shiva (Panch Kedar). These are: Kedarnath, Madhyamaheshwar, Tungnath, Rudranath and Kalpeshwar. There are five places of confluence of two rivers (Panch Prayag). These are Vishnuprayag (Dhaula Ganga and Alaknanda), Nandaprayag (Nandakini and Alaknanda), Karnaprayag (Pindar Ganga and Alaknanda), Rudraprayag (Mandakini and Alaknanda) and Devprayag (Bhagirathi and Alaknanda). At Devprayag, Bhagirathi and Alaknanda merge and the new river is called Ganga.

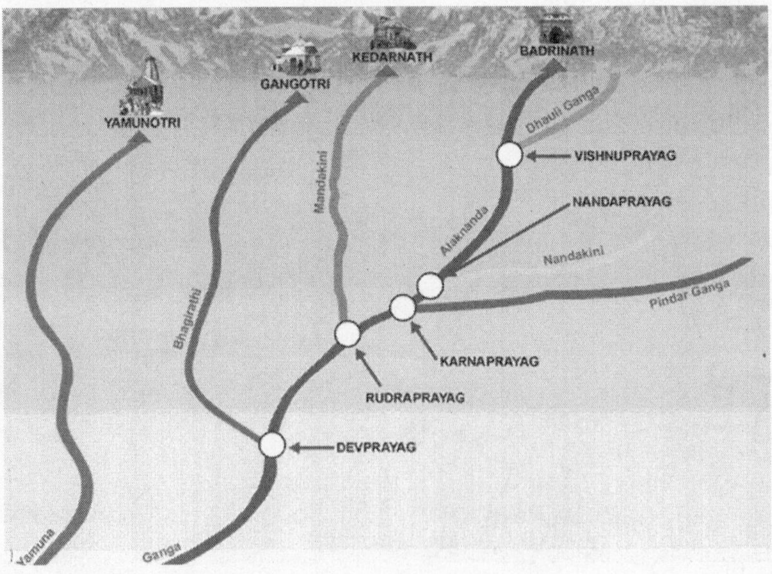

## Narmada flows from east to west

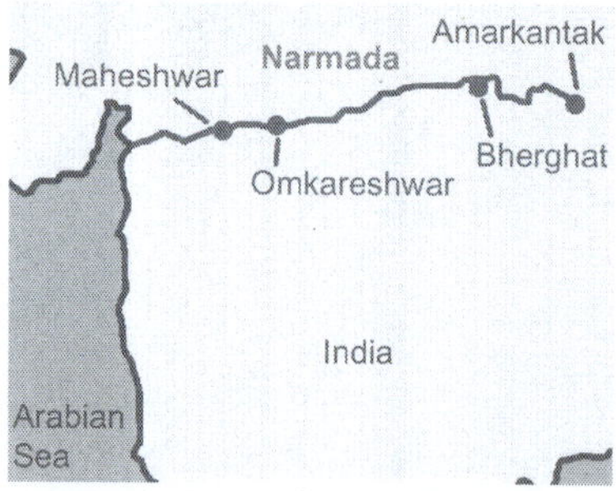


The origin of Narmada river is Narmada Kund, which is situated on the Amarkantak Hill in Anuppur District of East Madhya Pradesh. The river flows east to west, that is opposite to the direction of rotation of earth, over a length of 1,312 km before draining through the Gulf of Cambay (Khambat) into the Arabian Sea. It is the only rain-fed river in India that flows in a rift valley. The other two rain-fed rivers that flow from east to west are the Tapti and Mahi.

## Max Planck's life was dotted with tragedies

Max Karl Ernst Ludwig Planck was a German physicist who discovered quantum physics. He was the founder of quantum theory, for which he received the Nobel Prize in Physics in 1918. Planck's life was dotted with tragic occurrences. His first wife died early. His younger son died in World War I. He had twin daughters, one of which died during childbirth. The other twin married the husband of the first twin sister. They married and after two years she also died during childbirth. In 1944, when Planck was eighty-five, during World War II, a bomb fell on his house destroying all his documents, and a lifetime of accumulations. The next year, his only surviving son was executed after being caught in a conspiracy to assassinate Hitler.

## Congo crosses the equator twice

The Congo River, formerly known as the Zaire River, is also the deepest river of the world. It has a length of 4,700 km and arises in the highlands of East Africa and ends at the Atlantic Ocean. During the course of its journey, it crosses the equator twice.

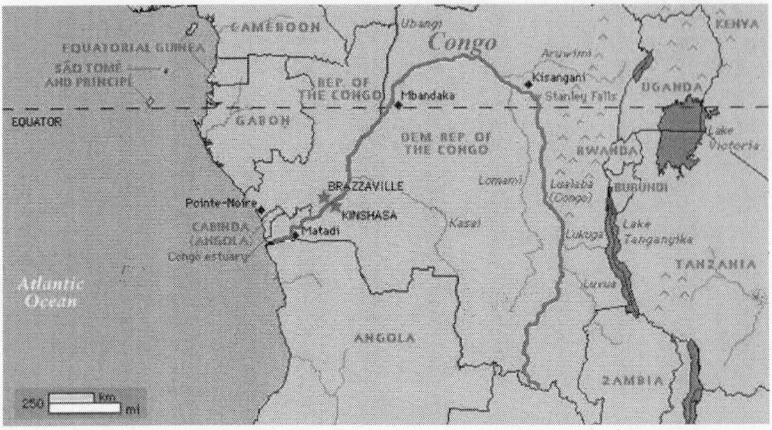


## The largest employer in the world is the Indian Railways in India

Indian Railways is one of the largest and busiest railway networks of the world that employs both long distance and suburban railway trains. It operates a total of about 8,702 trains transporting about 15 million passengers daily across 25 states. It has over 1.6 million people in its services.

## Windmills always turn anticlockwise

Windmills convert wind energy into mechanical energy that could be used for generating electricity or do mechanical work. The windmills are giant structures that have fans, which are designed in a similar fashion as the fans of aircrafts. The blades of the fans are such that they enable rotation in an anticlockwise direction. So most windmills of the world turn in an anticlockwise direction.

## Venetian blinds were invented in ancient Egypt

Venetian blinds are made of horizontal flat strips of vinyl joined together by corded pulleys that can either gather all the strips at the top or sides of the window, or simply let them loose to cover the window. The ancient Egyptians use strips of reed to create such blinds. The Chinese used bamboo strips for the same purpose. 'Venetian' blinds derive the name from Venice, where the Italian traders brought them from Persia.

## Sholay was inspired by Seven Samurai and The Magnificent Seven

The blockbuster Indian movie 'Sholay' was inspired by two movies 'Seven Samurai' and 'The Magnificent Seven'. 'The Magnificent Seven' was directed by John Sturges. The Hollywood film revolves around the seven men who are brought in from different parts of the world to save a village from the clutches of a bandit group. This film in turn was inspired by 'Seven Samurai' directed by Akira Kurosawa.

## Penguins walk upright. They swim but cannot fly

Penguins are aquatic birds that are found mostly in Antarctica. They are adapted to live in water and their wings have got modified into flippers. They can swim but cannot fly. On land they balance themselves upright using their tail and the flippers.

## Loktak Lake is the only floating lake in the world

The largest freshwater lake in northeastern India, the Loktak Lake, located near Moirang in Manipur, is also called the floating lake due to the floating *phumdis* (heterogeneous mass of vegetation, soil, and organic matters at various stages of decomposition) on it.

## 22 July is Pi Day

In every circle the circumference bears a constant ratio to its diameter. This constant is a transcendental number, denoted by the Greek alphabet $\pi$ (Pi). Pi is approximately equal to 22/7 or 3.14159. Pi Day is observed on July 22 (or 22/7 in day/month date format). Pi Day is also observed on March 14 (3.14 in month, date format) to commemorate the mathematical constant.

## 26th July is Kargil Day

Also known as Kargil Vijay Diwas, on this day in 1999, the Kargil conflict between India and Pakistan officially came to an end, when the Indian Army announced the complete eviction of Pakistani intruders. The Indian forces successfully took command of the outposts lost to the Pakistani Army.

## On 29th July, 1911 Mohun Bagan Club lifted the IFA Shield as the first Indian Team playing barefoot against East Yorkshire Regiment

The ground was hard and dry. A very pacy game commenced. The barefooted Bagan players matched their British counterparts in every aspect of the game. It was the 87th minute. Abhilash Ghosh received a pass from the captain, and his powerful shot went straight into the goal! This win was seen as a significant event at a time when Bengal was just partitioned by the British into East Bengal and West Bengal, and the Capital was shifted from Kolkata to Delhi. It marked a mass upheaval of the Indian natives against the British regime.

## Mosquitoes have 47 teeth

The proboscis of a mosquito needs to be inserted into the skin to draw blood. However, the proboscis cannot do it without any tool, and so it is equipped with 47 cutting tools, similar to incisors in animals, which help the mosquito pierce the proboscis into the skin.

## When the moon is directly overhead, you weigh slightly less

The moon exerts a pull on you when it is directly overhead, which cancels the gravitation pull of the earth on you slightly and therefore you weigh slightly less. Your mass, however remains the same.

## The African river Niger has its source close to its mouth

The Niger River in Africa is one of the world's longest rivers traversing 4,168 km. It has an unusual geography having a boomerang shape with the northern part named the 'Niger Bend'. The source is the Guinea Highlands and the river drains into the Atlantic ocean. Interestingly, the source and the mouth of the river are separated by just 240 km.

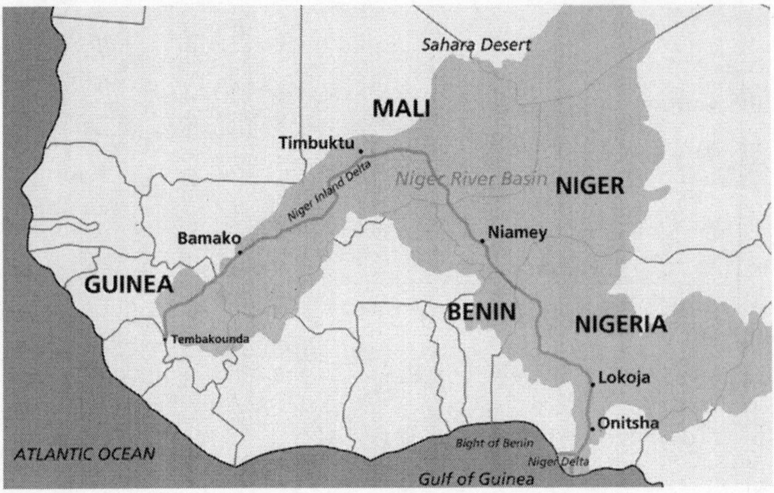


## Lord Byron was an all round sportsperson

Lord Byron, also known as George Gordon Byron, 6th Baron Byron, was a famous English poet. He was known to enjoy adventure. He was extremely fond of exercise and sports. He loved swimming and once swam from Sestos in Modern Gallipoli in European Turkey to Abydos in Upper Egypt. He mastered a wide variety of sports. In addition to swimming, he fenced, sculled, rode and shot at targets. At Harrow he was considered a good enough cricketer to play for the first team against Eton. He was also the captain of Harrow in that match.

## The module 'Eagle' of Apollo 11 had 20 seconds of fuel left when it landed on the moon

Apollo 11 was the mission of NASA, which placed a human on a celestial body, the moon. The journey to the moon took three and a half days and carried three astronauts: Neil Armstrong, Edwin Aldrin and Michael Collins. Armstrong said later 'We landed with a little less fuel than we would have liked to have had, maybe 20 seconds of fuel left.' Armstrong and Aldrin stepped on the moon and Armstrong uttered the famous words 'That's one small step for man, one giant leap for mankind.' After about two hours of moonwalking they returned to the craft, which was named Eagle. They left an inscription that said *'Here Men From The Planet Earth First Set Foot Upon the Moon, July 1969 A.D. We Came in Peace For All Mankind.'*

## Thomas Alva Edison, the inventor of the light bulb, was afraid of dark

Thomas Alva Edison is one of the greatest innovators who is credited with inventing the phonograph, the motion picture camera, film projectors, practical use of electricity, and an improved and effective electric light bulb, that was superior to gas lighting. When asked once if he were afraid of anything he replied 'I am afraid of the dark.'

## The 15th of March was called the 'Ides of March' in the Roman calendar.

The term 'Ides' was used for the 15th day of the months of March, May, July and October. The Ides of March was a festive day. However, the term 'Ides of March' is best known as the date on which Julius Caesar was killed in 44 B.C.

## The first fax machine was patented in 1843, i.e., 33 years before Alexander Graham Bell had demonstrated the telephone

The fax machine was invented by a Scottish inventor Alexander Bain in 1843. He devised an apparatus comprising two pins that were connected to two pendulums through five wires. When an electric signal was sent from the transmitting end, the receiving end was able to reproduce the signal on an electrochemically sensitive paper impregnated with chemicals. Thirty-three years later, Alexander Graham Bell invented the telephone.

## The popular programming language COBOL was invented by Admiral Grace Hopper, the first female admiral in the US Navy

Admiral Grace Murray Hopper was the first US navy officer and a computer scientist. She realized that with an easy programming language it would be easy for users who were neither mathematicians nor computer experts. This conviction led her to invent a popular programming language COBOL (COmmon Business-Oriented Language), which is used in business and finance.

## The longest word in any of the major English language dictionaries is pneumonoultramicroscopicsilicovolcano-coniosis

It refers to a lung disease contracted from the inhalation of very fine silica particles, specifically from a volcano; medically, it is the same as silicosis.

## The minimum number of satellites needed to show your position on the GPS device is 3

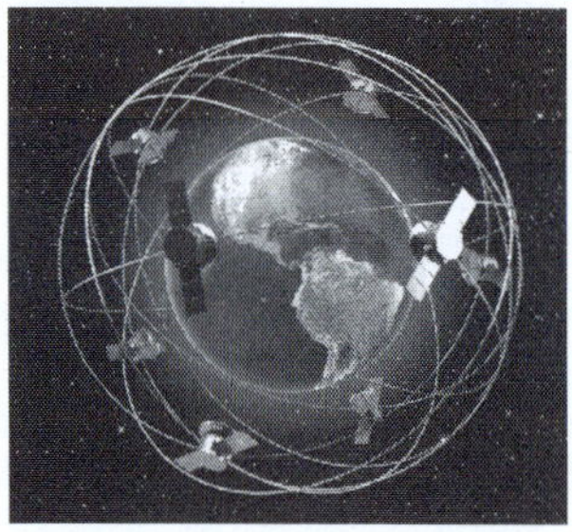

The Global Positioning System (GPS) is a system that uses satellites to point out the position of any object on the earth. The GPS uses a minimum of three satellites to indicate your position. A signal from one GPS satellite will just tell your distance from that particular satellite. However, three satellites are needed because space is three dimensional and the method of trilateration is used by the three satellites to compute your location.

## Hens that lay brown eggs have red ear lobes

The colour of the eggs depend upon the pigments that the egg encounters during its journey from a hen's oviduct. The colour of the pigment depends upon the hen's genetic composition. Incidentally, the original eggs laid were all brown. For many years humans started selecting hens that produced white eggs. The brown eggs have been reintroduced recently. The colour of the ear lobes also depends on the genetic composition of the hen and the hens with red ear lobes lay brown eggs.

## The 'pound' (#) key on your keyboard is called an octothorp

The term 'octothorp' was used as early as the 1960s in the Bell Labs, when they started experimenting on the touch tone dialing telephones. This symbol was used on the key and since it has eight points, it was called 'octo'.

## The total lunar eclipse that took place on Wednesday, June 16, 2011, was the longest lunar eclipse in a decade

A total lunar eclipse occurs when the Earth blocks all direct sunlight from reaching the Moon. There could be partial lunar eclipses occurring in a year too. The number of lunar eclipses in a single year can range from 0 to 3. On June 16, 2011, a total lunar eclipse occurred, which was visible for over 100 minutes in different parts of Asia, Europe and Africa. The partial eclipse lasted for 3 hours and 40 minutes, making it the longest total lunar eclipse in this decade.

## If an item moves very very fast, it becomes smaller and heavier

When an object moves very fast, it gains mass, but this effect is appreciable when the object moves at a speed very close to the speed of light, which is very very fast. In fact, the mass increases so much that it appears to be infinitely heavy. This is not observed in daily life but has been proven in the laboratory. Similarly, its length gets shortened when it moves with a very high speed.

## Swami Vivekananda penned the poem 'To the Fourth of July' on 4$^{th}$ July, 1898 commemorating the Independence Day of America. Exactly after four years, he passed away on the 4$^{th}$ of July, 1902

Swami Vivekananda was born as Narendranath Datta in January 12, 1863. He was an avid scholar of Western and Hindu Philosophy. He is one of the most admired spiritual leaders all over the world who left an indelible mark in history with his teachings. He celebrated the American Day of Independence on 4$^{th}$ July by penning the poem 'To the Fourth of July' and having it read specifically on the 4$^{th}$ of July, 1901. He passed away exactly a year later on 4$^{th}$ July, 1902.

## Deep Blue's chess playing program is capable of evaluating 100 million positions per second

Deep Blue is a computer designed by the International Business Machines Corporation (IBM). It was programmed to play chess. Deep Blue's chess playing program is written in C and runs under AIX operating system. It is capable of evaluating 100 million positions per second. In 1996, it was defeated by Gary Kasparov, and in 1997, an upgraded version of Deep Blue defeated Kasparov.

## Pearls melt in vinegar

A pearl is made of mostly calcium carbonate, which can react with a weak acid. Vinegar is a weak acid (acetic acid), which dissolves the calcium carbonate in the pearl and converts it into calcium, water and carbon dioxide.

## The longest place-name found in any English-speaking country is 85 alphabets long

The name of a place which is 85 alphabets long is called Taumatawhakatangihangakoauauotamateaturipukakapiki maungahoronukupokaiwhenuakitanatahu. It has longer versions of 92 and 105 letters too. It means 'The summit where Tamatea, the man with the big knees, the climber of mountains, the land-swallower who travelled about, played his nose flute to his beloved brother.' It is a hill located in New Zealand.

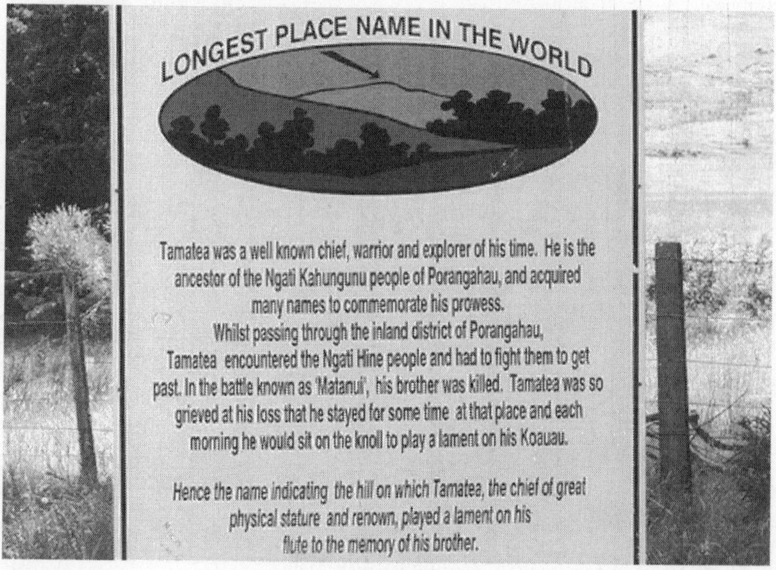


## StarCraft is the first computer game to be played in space

StarCraft was developed by Blizzard Entertainment and released for Microsoft Windows in 1998. The game is about three species who fight for dominance. The mission specialist of the space shuttle mission STS-96, a StarCraft fan, took a CD of the game with him to space. After orbiting the Earth 153 times and travelling 3.5 million nautical miles, the CD now is housed at Blizzard's home office.

## Mark Twain was born as Halley's comet passed by the earth and vowed to die with the comet's return in 75 years – and he did

Samuel Langhorne Clemens, better known as Mark Twain was a famous American writer and a humourist. He was born on November 30, 1835, when Halley's comet passed by the earth. He predicted that he would 'go out with it' and sure enough he passed away the next morning of April 21, after the Halley's comet passed by the earth after 75 years on April 20, 1910.

## Gurudev Rabindranath Tagore loved pies, patties, roasts and kebabs

Gurudev loved good food. He was such a foodie that he would often bring back recipes from his travels abroad with him so that these could be tried out at the Jorasanko kitchen. He has given elaborate accounts in his writings of the lunches and dinners that were hosted in countries like France, Italy, Turkey and Japan.

## Oscars given out during World War II were made of plaster because metal was in short supply

From 1942 until the end of World War II, Oscars were made out of plaster to conserve metal. After the war, the winners received 'real' replacement statues. Only one wooden Oscar was ever given in 1938, when ventriloquist Edgar Bergen received a wooden Oscar for his work with his wooden dummy, Charlie McCarthy.

## Walt Disney, the creator of Mickey Mouse began his career as a newspaper ad designer

In his life, Walt Disney experienced a lot of failures; he was rejected by the Army, struggled to find work after World War I, and worked for newspapers and movie theatres, struggled to start his own business before finally becoming one of the most successful entertainment entrepreneurs in the world.

## Tycho Brahe had an artificial silver nose

Tycho Brahe, a 16th century astronomer, lost the bridge of his nose in a duel with one of his friends over a mathematical computation. He wore a silver, gold and copper replacement nose for the rest of his life!

## There is enough lead in an average pencil to draw a line (35 miles) 56 km long

The chemical lead was used by the Romans as lead rods to write on papyrus. These rods left a grey mark just like graphite. Hence graphite was believed to be a type of lead. In 1564 a graphite deposit was discovered in England, which led to its widespread use for writing. The lead used in pencils are not actually the chemical lead but graphite and clay. An average pencil can write about 45,000 words, or a line about 35 miles (56 km) long.

## Minus 40 degrees Celsius is exactly the same as minus 40 degrees Fahrenheit

To convert from Celsius to Fahrenheit, multiply the Celsius value by 9 and divide the product by 5. To this obtained value, add 32. Therefore, –40 Celsius is equal to –40 × 9 = –360; –360 ÷ 5 = –72; –72 + 32 = –40 degrees Fahrenheit.

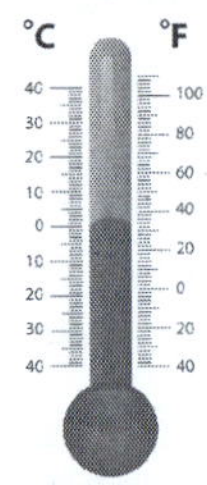


## The world's highest cricket ground is in Chail, Himachal Pradesh

Chail is located 49 km from Shimla. It is said that Maharaja Bhupinder Singh of Patiala was incensed when Lord Kitchener refused him entry to Shimla. The Maharaja built his summer capital at Chail. The cricket loving Maharaja built a cricket ground in 1893 after leveling a hilltop. This cricket pitch is 2,444 metres above sea level, making it the world's highest cricket ground.

## English kings did not speak English for 300 years

In January 1066, at the Battle of Hastings, William, Duke of Normandy, France, conquered England. For the next 300 years, the rulers and nobility of England spoke French, not English.

## The oldest and largest clearly visible meteorite crater site in the world is the Vredefort Dome in Free State, South Africa

About two billion years ago a meteorite, which was about ten kilometres in diameter hit an area near the town of Vredefort Dome near Johannesburg in South Africa. The impact of that meteorite created a crater that is 380 km across! Among the earth's 130 meteorite crater sites Vredefort Dome is the top third and is considered a World Heritage Site.

## 22 March is World Water Day

The United Nations General Assembly designated 22 March of each year as the World Water Day. It is held annually to focus attention on the importance of freshwater and advocate for the sustainable management of freshwater resources.

## If the 1$^{st}$ day of a month is a Sunday, the 13$^{th}$ of the same month falls on a Friday

If 1$^{st}$ is a Sunday then 8$^{th}$ is also a Sunday, because $8 = 1 + 7$. Then 9$^{th}$, 10$^{th}$, 11$^{th}$ and 12$^{th}$ are respectively Monday, Tuesday, Wednesday and Thursday. Hence 13$^{th}$ is Friday. If one considers 'Friday, the 13$^{th}$' to be a bad omen, one should not be happy with the first day of the month being a Sunday, thus a holiday.

## Gallium is a metal, which melts on palm of the hand

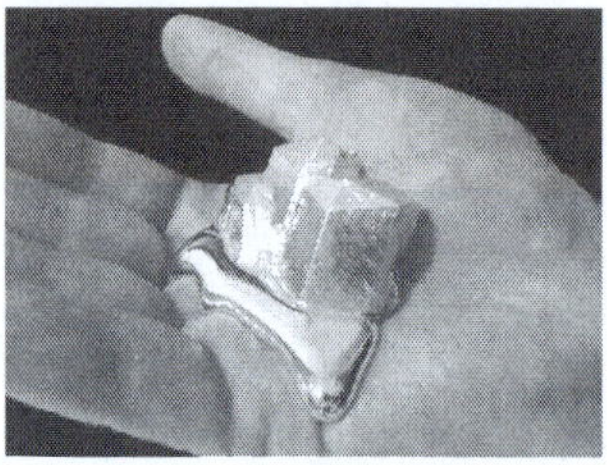

Gallium is a soft and brittle metal, which is found in bauxite or zinc ores. It melts at 29.7 degrees celsius, which is about room temperature. In fact, if you hold Gallium in your hand, it will melt. Gallium is mostly used in microwave technology.

## Bruce Lee was so fast that they actually had to slow a film down so you could see his moves

Most martial art films are sped up to make fighting scenes appear fast, it was the opposite of the norm in the case of Bruce Lee's films. His actions were very fast and could not be captured on the regular 24 frames per second (fps) and so his moves had to be filmed at 32 fps, and run the film slower so that one could see his moves.

## The fear of peanut butter sticking to the roof of the mouth is called Arachibutyrophobia

The word 'arachibutyrophobia' is derived from arachis meaning peanuts. The full meaning of the word is fear of peanuts sticking to the roof of the mouth. Arachis is a kind of oil found in many nuts and peanuts which stick to the roof of the mouth. In many cases the saliva fails to dissolve this and a person is not able to extract the sticky thing, and thus faces embarrassment, especially in public places and develops a fear for it.

## The first practical helicopter was invented in 1936. It was called the German Focke-Wulf Fw 61

Prof. Heinrich Focke, a German inventor devised the first practical helicopter called the Focke-Wulf Fw 16, which was successfully flown in 1936. By 1937 it set many world records, such as flying at an altitude of 800 feet. It could be flown by a pilot after only one hour of pilot briefing.

## India is the birthplace of chess

The original word for 'chess' is the Sanskrit *chaturanga*, meaning 'four members of an army'—which were most likely elephants, horses, chariots, and foot soldiers. According to a German Indologist researching on the origin of chess, in the 6$^{th}$ century, the Maukhari rulers of Kannauj, Uttar Pradesh used to play *chaturanga* with 16 cabinet terracotta before venturing into military campaigns. Historical accounts say during the later Gupta period there was an Indian army school where cadets were taught about warfare through terracotta pieces on *ashtapada*, which was again the game of chess in its primitive stage.

## The first recorded cricket test match was played on July 26, 1745.

World's first recorded test match was played between two teams of women. It was played in Surrey, England that year between Bramley and Hambledon villages. The Bramley team sported white dress and blue ribbons while the Hambledon team wore white dress and red ribbons. This report appeared in 'The Reading Mercury' on July 26, 1745.

## The web of a spider is a trap and not its home

A spider's web is not a home, but rather a trap for its food. It is woven by the spider using spider silk produced by special glands in their abdomen. The webs are as unique as snowflakes, with no two ever being the same. Some tropical spiders have built webs over 5.5 m across.

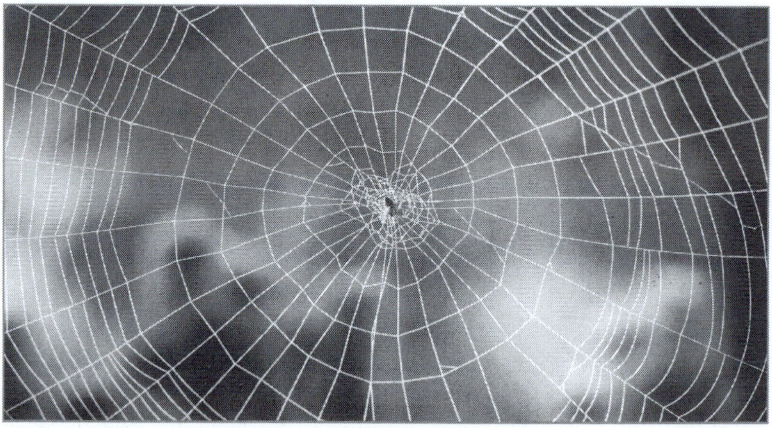

## 'Rocketgrams' were launched in India in 1930s to deliver mails and parcels

Rocketgrams or mails delivered by firing crude rockets towards their destinations was launched by Stephen Hector Taylor Smith of Indian Airmail Society in 1930s. The first successful dispatch was of two chickens, Adam and Eve across the Damodar river in Burnpur in West Bengal.

## Sharks are more ancient than dinosaurs

Sharks are fishes which have cartilages rather than bones. These fishes evolved earlier than dinosaurs, which were reptiles. The fossil records show that the shark existed about 400 million years ago. Dinosaurs were found during the Triassic period, i.e., about 225 million years ago.

## Bhutan issued a stamp in 1973 that looked like a record

Bhutan issued a stamp that was in fact a mini record and actually would play the Bhutanese national anthem if placed on a record player. It is made of thin plastic with a removable back to expose the adhesive. This stamp is much sought after by stamp collectors all over the world.

## The longest word that can be made using the letters only on one row of the keyboard is TYPEWRITER

It is indeed an interesting coincidence that the longest word is 'TYPEWRITER', which can be created with letters on the first row of the keyboard.

## The space between your eyebrows is called the glabella

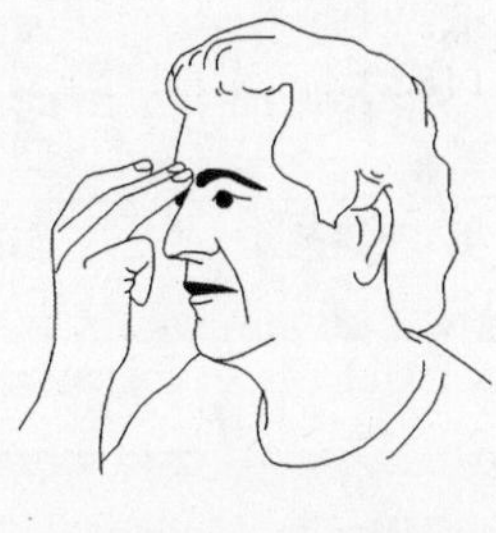

The glabella is the projecting space between the two eyebrows, just above the nose. It is triangular in shape. The name is derived from the Latin word *glabellus*, meaning smooth.

## The earliest cotton in the world was spun and woven in India

Since ancient times cotton cloth was spun in India with matchless skill. It is said that Roman emperors would wear delicate cotton from India, which they would call 'woven winds.' Moghul emperors called the fabrics 'morning dew' and 'cloth of running water.'

## The tallest mountain in the world could be Mauna Kea in Hawaii

The dormant volcano Mauna Kea (on the Big Island of Hawaii) could be considered the tallest mountain in the world. If you measure it from its base in the Hawaiian Trough (6,035 m) to its summit of 4,205 m, it reaches a height of 10,240 m.

## The one millionth digit of pi is a one

The value of pi is represented as 3.1415 or 22/7. However, pi is a transcendental number, which means that it is a non-terminating, non-recurring decimal. Mathematicians have used computers to calculate the value of pi to millions of digits. The millionth digit after the decimal has been calculated and found to be the number '1'.

## The only south east Asian country that has never been colonized by a western power is Thailand

The Kingdom of Thailand in South East Asia has one of the longest monarchies in history. After a revolution in 1932 a constitutional monarchy was established in Thailand. Throughout its history, Thailand was never colonized by any western power.

## The country with lowest elevation is Maldives

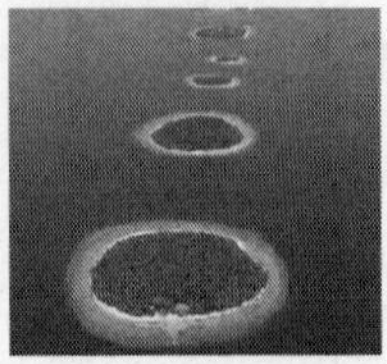

The country of Maldives is located in the Indian Ocean. It is an archipelago or a collection of 26 atolls or coral islands, out of which 5 to 10 are inhabited. It has an elevation of only 2.4 metres or 8 feet.

## Bradman was out for a duck in his last Test match against England

In this last test match, Bradman came out to the crease amidst a thunderous ovation, which lasted several minutes. Hollies was to write later, 'I don't think Don saw it properly. He seemed to have tears in his eyes'. Bradman wrote in Farewell to Cricket, 1950, 'That reception had stirred my emotions very deeply and made me anxious – a dangerous state of mind for any batsman to be in. I played the first ball from Hollies, though not sure I really saw it. The second was a perfect length googly which deceived me'. Bradman missed a Test total of 7,000 runs by just 4 runs; it would have given him a Test career average of 100, instead of 99.94.

## The Kumbh Mela is a huge Hindu religious festival that takes place in India every 12 years

In 2001, more than 60 million people attended the Kumbh Mela in Prayag, Allahabad, breaking the record for the world's biggest gathering. The mass of people was photographed from space by the Indian satellite IRS-ID. The satellite imagery of January 15 gave a clear glimpse of the mela site. A striking aspect was that the camera could capture all the 300 blocks/sectors/camps where milling crowds of pilgrims were present.

## Galileo, considered as the pride of Italy, was prohibited by the Church from looking through the telescope after dark

The Church held the belief that the earth was the centre of the Universe and the Church had all the power. When Galileo was found to observe the night sky through his telescope, the Church was alarmed that he might discover something that would question the beliefs and the power of the Church.

## The world's largest flower is the *Rafflesia arnoldii*

*Rafflesia arnoldii* is a rare flower found in the rainforests of Indonesia. It has an unpleasant smell of decaying flesh. It can grow to be 0.9 m across and weigh up to 6.8 kg and is considered the world's largest flower.

## The full name of the City of Bangkok is Krungtheph phramahanakhonbowonratakosinmahintharayuthay amahadilokphiphobnovpharadradchataniburiromudo msantisug.

The name translates to 'City of Angels, Great City and Residence of the Emerald Buddha, Impregnable City of Lord Indra, Grand Capital of the World, Endowed with nine precious gems, Abounding in Enormous Royal Places which resemble the Heavenly Abode where reigns the Reincarnated God, a city given by Indra and built by Vishnukarm'.

## Ada Lovelace was the world's first computer programmer

Ada Lovelace, the English Mathematician, and daughter of Lord Byron, was chiefly known for her work on Charles Babbage's analytical machine, or the computer. She worked on the engine with notes of her own which are recognized today and the world's first computer programme.

## February 21 is observed as the International Mother Language Day

This day is being observed every year since February 2000 to promote linguistic and cultural diversity and multilingualism. The date represents the day in 1952 when students demonstrating for recognition of their language, Bangla, as one of the two national languages of the then East Pakistan, were shot and killed by police in Dhaka, the capital of what is now Bangladesh. Thus it was called the 'Bangla Bhasha Divas' and with the UN resolution in 2000, it came to be known as the International Mother Language Day.

## The Himalayan mountains are growing at the rate of 2.5 cm a year

The Himalayas—from the Sanskrit *hima*, meaning 'snow,' and *alaya*, meaning 'abode'—are the world's highest mountain range that lie in the north of India. They extend (2400 km). The mountain range is slowly growing taller, by almost an inch (2.5 cm) a year.

## The Tonle Sap River in Cambodia flows north for almost half the year and then south for the rest of the year

The Tonle Sap River is a combination of a freshwater lake and a river. It originates from the lake and flows to the Mekong River in the north from November to May. However, with the arrival of rains during the monsoon season, the Mekong River swells up, pushing the waters of the Tonle Sap River back to the freshwater lake. The Tonle Sap River has been designated as an ecological hotspot.

## Earth is referred to as the Blue Planet

Earth has about 70 per cent of its water distributed in the oceans, which is observed from the space. This water, combined with the atmosphere makes the earth appear blue from space.

## An African woman's risk of dying from pregnancy related causes is one in 16, in Asia, it is one in 65. In Europe, it is one in 1,400

Every year, one woman dies every minute from pregnancy related causes, with a majority of women dying in the developing countries. The developed countries, such as Europe, the women have access to a good medical care infrastructure and the death rate is much lower.

## Construction workers' hard hats were first invented and used in the building of the Hoover Dam

The construction workers' hats were invented by E.W. Bullard, who was inspired by the steel helmets he wore during the World War I. He devised what is now known as Hard Hats. They were called so because they were made by steaming canvas and glue to make a hard material, which were then fashioned into hats. When the Hoover Dam was being constructed in 1931, the companies insisted their workers wore these hats for safety.

## The city of Kolkata has been the main working place of five nobel laureates

The nobel laureates are: Ronald Ross – Physiology or Medicine (1902), Rabindranath Tagore – Literature (1913), C.V. Raman – Physics (1930), Mother Teresa – Peace (1979), and Amartya Sen – Economic Sciences (1998).

## Hot water freezes faster than cold water

This phenomenon is called the Mpemba effect. Under the same cooling circumstances the hot water cools faster than the cold water. Scientists have provided several explanations for this. The surface temperature of the hot water becomes supercooled allowing the water to cool evenly. In case of cold water, ice sheet forms on top, thus insulating the rest of the water from cooling fast. There are no dissolved gas bubbles in the heated water, as in cold water, which allows the hot water to freeze quickly.

## The circle is a regular polygon of infinite number of sides

A triangle has three sides, a square has four, and if you continue to increase the number of sides, you will get different kinds of polygons. In the limit of number of sides tending to infinity, you will get a circle.

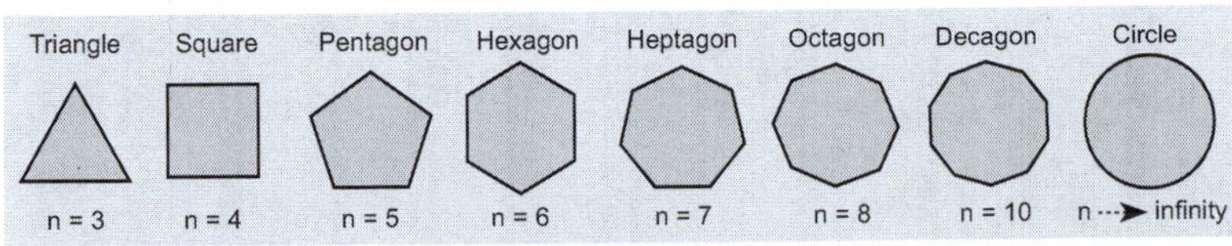


## The banyan tree is the national tree of India

The banyan, or Indian fig tree (*Ficus benghalensis*), is considered a symbol of immortality and is mentioned in many Indian myths and legends. This self-renewing plant is India's national tree. The tree can grow up to several hectares using its prop roots, which grow down from the tree trunk into woody structures.

## Ancient Indians contributed significantly to the knowledge of mathematics

Indians made significant contributions to calculus, trigonometry and algebra. The decimal system was invented in India in 100 B.C. The concept of zero as a number is also attributed to India. The ancient Indian mathematicians also developed the concept of negative numbers.

## Another way to say 'every 9 years' is Novennial

Novennial is a Latin term containing two words; *novennis* meaning nine, and *annus* meaning year. It means something done every ninth year or something recurring every ninth year.

## Baikal Lake in Russia is the deepest lake in the world

Lake Baikal is situated in the South East Siberia in Russia. It is one of the richest and diverse repositories of flora and fauna. The depth of Baikal Lake is 5,315 feet making it the deepest lake in the world.

## In India February 28th is celebrated as National Science Day

This day, in the year 1928, Sir Chandrashekhara Venkata Raman announced to the world his famous discovery, the Raman Effect, a discovery which would earn him the Nobel Prize. Raman sought to find the explanation of the anomalies in scattering of light by molecules, and in 1928, he made the unexpected and highly surprising discovery that a change in the wavelength of light occurs when a light beam is deflected by molecules. The scattered light showed not only the radiation that was derived from the primary light but also a radiation that contained other wavelengths, which were foreign to the primary light. This phenomenon was named the Raman effect.

## The general condition of colour blindness is called Daltonism

The term 'Daltonism' is after the English Chemist John Dalton, who published the first scientific paper on colour blindness after realizing he was colour blind himself. The test used to identify colour blindness is called the Ishihara test.

## Rain drops are not tear-shaped but look like hamburger buns

It was generally believed that rain drops were tear-shaped. Raindrops are round when they are formed. As they start falling they change their shape. Scientists with high-speed cameras have discovered that raindrops become like the top of a burger in shape. This is due to high air flow at the bottom of the drop resulting in low surface tension and subsequent flattening out of the drop.

## Gurudev Rabindranath Tagore contributed towards the national anthems of three countries

The First Asian Nobel laureate, Gurudev Rabindranath Tagore wrote the national anthems of India (*Jana Gana Mana*) and Bangladesh (*Amar Sonar Bangla*). The Sri Lankan national anthem (*Sri Lanka Matha*) was written by Ananda Samarakoon in 1940 who was in Shantiniketan in 1936. He was very much influenced by Rabindranath Tagore and this got reflected in the Sri Lankan national anthem.

## India is one of the world's largest tea producers

Tea (*chai*) is the most popular beverage the world over. Tea (*Camellia sinensis*) originated in China, and the modern form of tea taken with milk was developed by the British in India. The British developed many tea gardens in Assam and Darjeeling in the nineteenth century and today India leads in tea technology.

## The international telephone dialing code for Antarctica is 672

Antarctica has four bases with their own city dialing codes. The city code of Casey Base is 12, Davis Base is 10, Macquarie Base is 13 and Mawson Base is 11. To dial Antarctica, say from India, you will have to dial the International exit code, which is +91 for India, followed by 672, the city code and the phone number at Antarctica.

## The place with the most contrasting season is Verkhoyansk in Russia

Verkhoyansk is a place located in Siberia. During summer, the temperature is about 13 degrees celsius, with about 16 degrees celsius in July. In winter it is minus 45 degrees celsius. The difference between the two temperatures is about 60 degrees celsius.

## World Tourism Day is observed on September 27

On September 27, every year, people across the world observe the World Tourism Day. On this day in 1970, the United Nations World Tourism Organization adopted the statutes, which aimed at promoting tourism among the global community and understanding its social, cultural, political and economic value.

## The most densely populated country in the world is the Netherlands

Netherlands, located in the North Western Europe, is country of mills, bulb fields, dykes and canals. Also known as Holland, Netherland has a beautiful landscape. As per the data of March 2011 it had a population of 1,66,63,831 and 493 inhabitants per square km.

## The words 'abstemious' and 'facetious' both have all the five vowels in them in order

'Abstemious' means a habit that is moderate, especially in eating and drinking. 'Facetious' means joking. Both these words have the vowels a, e, i, o, u arranged in their order of natural occurrence.

## The Asian Continent covers 30 per cent of the total earth land area, but accounts for 60 per cent of the world's population

The Asian continent is home to 53 countries. The total area covered by it is 44,579,000 square kilometres. The continent covers about 30 per cent of the total land on earth. However, about 60 per cent of the world's population is found here with China and India leading with 2.5 billion people.

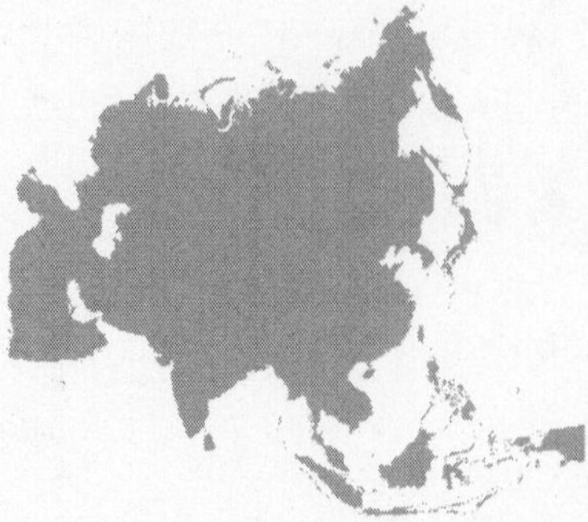

## English sailors were referred to as 'limeys'

In the $17^{th}$ and $18^{th}$ century, the British sailors suffered heavily from scurvy, a disease that occurred due to low vitamin C intake. Since the sailors were mostly at sea, fresh vegetables and fruits were not readily available to them. So they added lime juice to their diet to combat scurvy.

## The Peregrine falcon is the fastest bird on the planet

The Peregrine falcons have been used in the countries of Asia and Europe for falconry. This bird is a hunter and during its hunting stoop, it can dive at around 320 km per hour. The highest diving speed recorded so far is 390 km per hour, making it the fastest bird on earth.

## Montreal was named after a local mountain 'Mont Royal'

Montreal is an island city on the Lawrence River in Canada. It has a 213 m high mountain called the Mont Royal. It is said that Montreal was named after this mountain.

## More than a million Indians are millionaires, yet most Indians live on less than two dollars a day

According to an estimate by the World Wealth Report the number of millionaires would double by the year 2015. In contrast to this, an estimated 35% of India's population lives below the poverty line, with a per capita income of less than two dollars a day.

## There are roughly 4,000 known minerals, although only about 200 are of major importance

A mineral is a chemical compound that is formed due to geological processes. Every mineral is distinct from each other in terms of its structure and properties. There are about 4,000 known minerals and many new minerals are being discovered. However, only about 200 of them are used today for various purposes.

## The inability to identify people by their faces is called prosopagnosia

The term 'prosopagnosia' is derived from two Greek words; *prosopon* meaning face and *agnosia* meaning not knowing. Prosopagnosia is a condition where a person is unable to identify faces. The person might, however, be able to identify objects. It is also called 'face blindness' and is found in 2.5 per cent of the population.

## It takes about 8 minutes for light to travel from the Sun's surface to the earth

Sunlight is generated by the sun through nuclear reactions that take place in its core. The collisions of atoms result in gamma rays, which collide with matter and form the spectrum of electromagnetic radiation on reaching the sun's surface. It takes the light about 10,000 years to escape the sun's core to reach the surface. It takes about 8.3 minutes for this light to reach the earth.

## The word Cotton originates from the Arabic word 'Qutun'

Cotton was cultivated in the Indus Valley in India and Pakistan, and also in Mexico. The Indus valley cotton was very fine and was valued highly in the Middle East countries and Europe. The cultivation and manufacture of this fabric was taken up by the Arabs in 600 A.D. and they gave it the name 'qutun', which means 'fine textile'.

## Usain Bolt is the fastest man alive

Did you know that by the time you complete reading this sentence, Usain Bolt, the Jamaican sprinter, who won the Olympic Gold Medals for Men's 100 m race, 200 m race and the team event of 4 × 100 m relay race at the Beijing Olympics held in 2008, and London Olympics held in 2012, would have reached the finishing line of 100 m.

## A violin actually contains 70 separate pieces of wood

A violin has seventy parts. Each part is made of wood that determines the tone the violin will produce. The wood used for each part is also different and is obtained from different trees, such as spruce, maple and willow.

## Butterflies taste with their feet

Butterflies have sensors in their feet, which allow them to find out if the leaves are good enough to support the nutritional needs of their young ones. They can taste the leaves and other food with these sensors.

## India is the world's largest producer of dried beans

Beans are a very important source of proteins. India is one of the largest producers of beans, such as kidney beans and chickpeas.

## The Mauna Loa Volcano in Hawaii is the largest volcano on Earth

Mauna Loa, meaning 'Long Mountain' in Hawaii, is the world's largest volcano that rises about 4 kilometres above sea level. Its flanks go deep into the sea for about 5 kilometres and the pressure exerted by the mountain depresses the sea bed by another 8 kilometres. This makes the total height of the volcano to be about 17 kilometres.

## The thumbnail grows the slowest, and the middle nail grows the fastest

Our fingers vary in size. The middle finger is the longest followed by the second and the fourth fingers. The little finger and the thumb are smaller than the others. The nails grow from the cells at the root of the nail. They become keratinized and hardened as they grow. The nail of the middle finger grows the fastest and the thumbnail grows the slowest.

## India has the most number of mosques in the world

India has about 18 per cent of its population following Islam. The country has about 3,00,000 mosques, which is much more than that in the Muslim world.

## The watch was invented by Peter Henlein of Nuremberg in 1510

Peter Henlein was a locksmith in Nuremberg, Germany. He was the first person to devise a watch to read time. He produced small portable mechanical clocks that were encased in small drums or cans.

## The value of 'pi' used in mathematics was first calculated by the Indian mathematician Baudhayana

Baudhayana was a mathematician who lived in the $6^{th}$ century. He discovered what is now known as the Pythagorean theorem. While explaining the Pythagorean theorem, he accurately calculated the value of pi. He is also credited with formulating the first *sulba sutras*, that mathematical calculations on geometry.

## DNA was discovered in 1869 by Friedrich Miescher

Johannes Friedrich Miescher, a physiological chemist from Basel, Switzerland isolated nuclein, the material that contained the nucleic acids or de-oxyribonucleic acid (DNA) from the white blood cells in 1869.

## India's pastoral communities are largely dependent on dairy and have made India the largest milk-producing country in the world

India is the highest milk-producing country in the world with about 121 million tons of milk produced during 2010–11. About 40 per cent of Indian farmers own livestock and the collective livestock of India is about three times that of the United States of America.

## India is the largest democracy in the world

India is one of the oldest civilizations in the world. It is the 7th largest and the 2nd largest populated country. India is the largest (populous) democracy in the world and has six major parties and more than 40 regional parties.

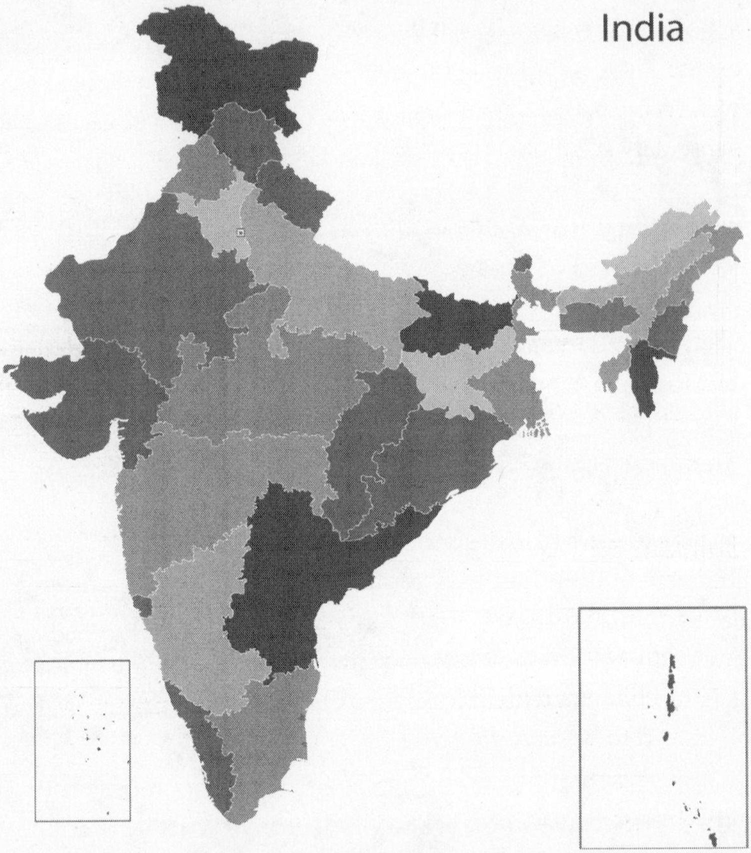


## 'Go' is the shortest complete sentence in the English language

The meaning of 'Go' in this case should be understood as an action verb used as a command, such as 'You Go'. However, even if 'You' is not used, the meaning is clear.

## The emperor of Japanese cinema, Akira Kurosawa was asked to sit separately from the other students in school

Akira Kurosawa was one of the eight children born to a family of samurai warriors. He came from a poor family and so the schools of the day discriminated against him. In the class he was asked to sit separately from other children.

## Christians and Jews have been living in India since 52 A.D. and 200 B.C., respectively

The first Jews were believed to have come to India in the 580 B.C., but the major wave of immigration of Jews from Jerusalem took place in the 70 A.D. Christianity was brought to India by Apostle Thomas, one of the disciples of Jesus in about 52 A.D.

## Jainism and Buddhism were founded in India

Gautama Buddha was the founder of Buddhism who was born in about 580 B.C. Mahavir Jain was born in about 599 B.C. and his teachings founded Jainism. Both Buddhism and Jainism are believed to have originated in the same century.

## It is illegal to take Indian currency (rupees) out of India

According to the rules set by the Reserve Bank of India, a person going out of India can take out with him Indian currency notes upto ₹ 5000 to any country other than Nepal or Bhutan, and any amount in denomination not exceeding ₹ 100 to Nepal or Bhutan.

## The highest bridge in the world is located in the Himalayan mountains

The Highest bridge lies in the Ladakh valley in Kashmir between Dras and Suru Rivers and is called the Bailey Bridge. The bridge measures about 30 metres and is about 5,600 metres above sea level.

## Most historians agree that the first recorded account of plastic surgery is found in ancient Indian Sanskrit texts

Plastic surgery is the practising of reshaping the body through medical surgery. Ancient texts such as the *Sushruta Samhita* describe the technique of rhinoplasty or the plastic surgery of the nose as early as 600 B.C.

## Teflon was discovered accidently

Scientist Dr. Roy Plunkett was conducting a coolant gas experiment in 1938 to make a new refrigerant. He mixed tetrafluoroethylene with hydrochloric acid and stored it in a coolant called dry ice. He found that a reaction had taken place and the compound that had formed was insoluble in almost everything; cold water, hot water, acetone, ethers, acids, and alcohols. It did not char or melt under a soldering iron, it didn't rot, swell, mildew, mold, or degrade in sunlight. He got a patent for the product in 1941.

## The total solar eclipse is a cosmic spectacle

The total solar eclipse of the $24^{th}$ October, 1995 almost coincided with the bicentenary of John Keats, known as the 'poet of beauty', who was born on $31^{st}$ October, 1795. Incidentally Keats wrote 'Beauty is truth, truth beauty'.

## The lowest dry point on earth is the Dead Sea in the Middle East is about 1,300 feet (400 metres) below sea level

The Dead Sea is a saline lake between the countries of Israel and Jordan. It is the deepest lake in the world with its shores at about 1,300 feet below the sea level. Since it is a hypersaline lake with about 35 per cent salinity, no fish or other marine life forms are found in it, except microscopic algae. Its mud yields raw material for cosmetics and fertilizers.

## Antarctica is the highest, driest, and coldest continent on Earth

The name 'Antarctica' in Greek means 'the opposite of Arctic'. Antarctica is located in the south pole and at 14.4 million $km^2$ is the fifth largest continent. Since it has little precipitation, it is the largest desert in the world.

## The world's population has increased by 3.1 billion in last 40 years

According to the United Nations, the world's population reached 7 billion on October 2011. In 1804, the world population was 1 billion. It became 2 billion in 1927, 3 billion in 1960, 4 billion in 1975, 5 billion in 1987, and 6 billion in 1999.

## The distance from the surface of Earth to the centre is about 6,378 kilometres

If a hole is dug down to the centre of the earth, then it would take a digging through about 6,378 kilometres to reach the centre of the Earth. However, since the earth is not a perfect sphere and flat at the poles, the distance from the poles to the centre of the earth would be lesser than that from the equator.

## The largest ocean of the world is the Pacific Ocean that covers nearly one-third of the Earth's surface

The Pacific Ocean has a total area of 1,55,557,000 square kilometres. Located between the Southern Ocean, Asia, Australia, and the western hemisphere it is the largest ocean covering nearly one-third of the earth's surface.

## The saltiest sea in the world is the Red Sea with 41 parts of salt per 1,000 parts of water

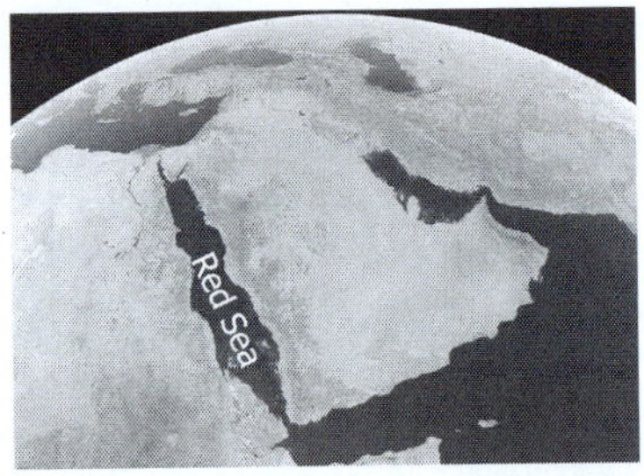


The Red Sea water is located in the subtropical region and there is a lot of evaporation from it. Further, the fresh water rivers that drain into it are also few, and so the salt in the water cannot get diluted. These factors cause the Red Sea water to contain high levels of salt.

## Earth is the only planet on which water can exist in liquid form on the surface

The temperature and atmospheric pressure support the liquid form of water on the earth's surface. Liquid water is important to support life on earth.

## Swami Vivekananda inspired the name of Ministry of Human Resources Development

The Education Ministry of India was renamed the Ministry of Human Resources Development after the ideology of 'Man-Making' or 'Human Resource' propounded by Swami Vivekananda. It happened in 1988 during the 125th birth anniversary of Swami Vivekananda. He was born on 12 January 1863.

## There are five years in a quinquennium

A quinquennium is a cycle or time period of five years taken together. It is derived from the latin word *quinque* meaning five and *annus* meaning years.

## The world's largest school is in Lucknow, India

The City Montessori School at Lucknow, India has the largest number of students. In 2008, it had 32,114 students. In 2010, it received a certificate from the Guinness Book of World Records saying it had a record enrolment of 39,437 students.

## Only 11 per cent of the earth's surface is used to grow food

The earth is covered with 29 per cent land and 71 per cent water. Of the 29 per cent land, a large part is covered by snow and ice. Out of the area left, there are grasslands and forests. About 11 per cent land is available for agriculture.

## Astronauts cannot belch

Belching is the release of gas from the digestive system through the mouth. Every time a person swallows food or liquid, a small amount of air goes into the stomach. This air forms gas bubbles in the stomach. The muscles in the food pipe relax to allow these bubbles to escape as burps. In space, the gas bubbles cannot rise to the top as there is no gravity to separate liquid from gas in their stomachs.

## Vincent van Gogh created his most dramatic works while at Asylum in Saint Remy, France

Vincent Willem van Gogh was a celebrated Dutch artist. In 1889, when he was 35 years old, he suffered bouts of depression, and got himself admitted to an Asylum in Saint Remy. There he created some of his famous paintings, such as 'Starry Starry Night', 'Olive Trees with the Alpilles in the Background', and 'Cypresses'.

## The coldest temperature ever measured on Earth was –129 Fahrenheit (–89 Celsius)

Vostok, Antarctica, is the most remote research stations at 1,300 km from the South Pole. On July 21, 1983 the researchers recorded the lowest temperature on earth here. It is the coldest inhabited area on Earth.

## India has the largest postal network in the world

There are about 1,55,669 post offices or outlets, of which roughly 89 per cent are outside the cities. On an average, one post office serves an area of 21.13 square km, and a population of 6,602 people.

## The longest navigable aqueduct in the world is the Magdeburg Water Bridge

The Magdeburg Water Bridge is a navigable aqueduct that has been built in Germany. It connects the Elbe-Havel Canal to the Mittellandkanal, crossing over the Elbe River. It is the longest aqueduct measuring 3,012 feet.

## Aluminium cans take 500 years to break down

The rate of break down depends on the decomposition environment. For example, the aluminium cans may decay in about 80 to 100 years when put in sea water. Aluminium cans can be recycled into cans, plates and many other articles.

## Olive trees can live for more than 1,000 years

Olive has been the symbol of peace for thousands of years. Their roots are spread really wide which enable them to survive drought conditions. A typical olive tree can live 1,000 years or more because the root can regenerate the entire tree if the original tree is destroyed.

## The World's largest hot desert is the Sahara in North Africa

The Sahara Desert is located in North Africa. At over 90,00,000 $km^2$ it is almost as large as the United States. Most of the Saharan landscape is parched with sand dunes and sand seas. There are several mountain ranges, which are volcanic.

## The warmest sea in the world is the Red Sea

The surface water temperature of Red Sea, the warmest in the world, in summer ranges from 26 degrees Celsius (79 degrees Fahrenheit) in the north portion to 30 degrees Celsius (86 degrees Fahrenheit) in the south portion.

## Mandarin Chinese is the most spoken language in the world

Mandarin Chinese is spoken by more than 1 billion speakers. It is the official language of China, Taiwan and one of the four official languages of Singapore. It is one of the six official languages of the United Nations. English is the second most spoken language with 512 million native speakers.

## The deepest hole ever made by humans is in Kola Peninsula in Russia, which was completed in 1989, creating a hole 12,262 metres (7.6 miles) deep

The Kola peninsula is in South West Russia, near Finland. In 1970 Russian geologists started drilling into the Peninsula to study the deep core of the earth. However, after 22 years of digging, work had to stop when the crust turned mushy under the drill, the underground rock was much hotter than expected at that depth. As a result of the digging, a super deep borehole was created, which is about 7.6 miles or 12.23 km deep.

## Omar Sharif, who acted in films like *Lawrence of Arabia* and *Mackenna's Gold* was quite a prolific Bridge player

Omar Sharif was attracted to the card game of Bridge when he was 21 years old. In 1964, he was the captain of the United Arab Republic team at the World Bridge Olympiad. With an aim to promote Bridge, he formed the Omar Sharif Bridge Circus in 1968, which extensively toured America and Canada. He quit Bridge in 2000.

## Shanghai, China is the most populous city in the world

Shanghai covers an area of 6,340 square kilometres. It is one of the world's largest seaports and a major industrial centre of China. It has a population of 13.3 million people making it the most populous city in the world.

## It takes the Hubble telescope about 97 minutes to complete an orbit of the Earth

The Hubble telescope was launched by NASA in 1990. Since then it has beamed thousands of pictures to earth giving us a magnificent view of the space beyond earth. It has helped determine the age of the universe, existence of dark energy and identity of quasars.

## 34 million people were killed in World War I

2014 happens to be the centenary of the first World War. 14 million people were killed in World War I and 20 million died in the flu epidemic that followed it.

## The gravity on Mars is 38 per cent of that found on Earth

Mars is smaller than Earth. Its density and mass is also lower than earth. Since all these factors are lower, its gravity is also lower than Earth. In fact, the gravity on Mars is 62 per cent lower than Earth, meaning the Martian gravity is 38 per cent of the gravity on Earth. So a 50 kg person on Earth would weigh 19 kg on Mars.

## About 70 per cent of the world's fresh water is stored as glacial ice

Glaciers are formed at the North and South Poles and in high mountains, such as the Himalayas. Glaciers are sometimes known as rivers of snow. The snow remains for more than a year and as more snow falls, the lower layers get compressed, forming ice. This ice is called glacial ice. Glacial ice can be more than 1,50,000 years old.

## In October 1999 an iceberg of the size of London broke free from the Antarctic ice shelf

This iceberg broke from the Antarctic ice shelf and floated towards the southernmost tip of Argentina. It travelled at the rate of 8 to 10 kilometres a day.

## Every second around 100 lightning bolts strike the earth

Lightning bolts are electric discharges that originate in the clouds during a storm and travel to the earth's surface. Every second, about 100 lightning bolts strike the earth and each bolt can contain one billion volts of electricity.

## Less than one per cent of water on earth is available to us for use

Only 3 per cent water of the earth is fresh, rest 97 per cent salted. Of that 3 per cent, over 2 per cent is frozen in ice sheets and glaciers. It means less than 1 per cent fresh water is found in lakes, rivers and underground. Water, indeed is a scarce resource.

## The speed of light is equal to 1,86,287.49 miles or 29,97,92,458 m per second

Light travels at the fastest speed. The speed of light, measured in vacuum is found to be 29,97,92,458 metres per second or 1,86,287.49 miles per second. This value is generally rounded off to 186,000 miles per second.

## The first satellite capable of relaying telephone and satellite TV signals was named the Telstar

In 1962 Telstar was developed by AT&T and it was placed at an orbit of 682 to 4,030 miles (i.e. 1,091 to 6,444 km) orbiting the earth in 2 hours 40 minutes. The first transatlantic television signals were transmitted through Telstar. With the launch of Telstar, wireless communications, such as voice, television, fax and data transfer were carried out between UK, Brazil, France, Italy and the US.

## Christian Barnard performed the first ever heart transplant

Dr. Christian Barnard was the first person in the world to perform the open heart surgery in 1967. He transplanted the heart of a young accident victim on to a 59 year old man Mr. Louis Washkansky. Mr. Washkansky lived for 18 days and died of pneumonia.

## The eyelids are the fastest moving muscle of the human body

The fastest moving muscle in the human body is the one that closes the eyelid. This muscle is called the orbicularis muscle. The opening or closing of the eye, or the blink of the eye was used for measuring time in ancient India. The Vedic texts designated the blink of an eye as a *nimesh*. One *nimesh*, according to the modern mathematical calculations, is 0.2133 seconds.

## Alfred Nobel invented dynamite in 1866

Alfred Nobel was a Swedish industrialist, engineer and inventor. He was into construction and that led him to perform experiment to find out ways of blasting rocks. His research led him to nitroglycerine. He found out that mixing silica with nitroglycerine would make it easy to handle. This mixture is known today as the dynamite.

## Wilhelm Röntgen won the first Nobel Prize for physics for discovering X-rays

Wilhelm Conrad Röntgen was a German physicist. In 1895 he was working with cathode rays when he discovered a different kind of electromagnetic radiation. Since the radiation was unknown at that time, he called it the X-rays. He received the first Nobel Prize in physics in 1901 for this discovery.

## The tallest tree ever was an Australian eucalyptus – in 1872 it was measured at 435 feet, that is about 133 metres tall

The *Eucalyptus regnans* trees of Australia are among the tallest trees in the world. They can reach up to the heights of 100 metres or more. The most widely known tallest tree to be measured is called the Ferguson tree, named after the surveyor William Ferguson who measured the fallen tree to be 132.6 metres, that too after the top was broken off.

## The Ebola virus kills 4 out of every 5 humans it infects

The deadly Ebola virus was first reported in Zaire in 1978. It spreads through the blood and causes hemorrhage in all organs. Internal bleeding results in shock and death. There are no drugs or vaccines against this disease.

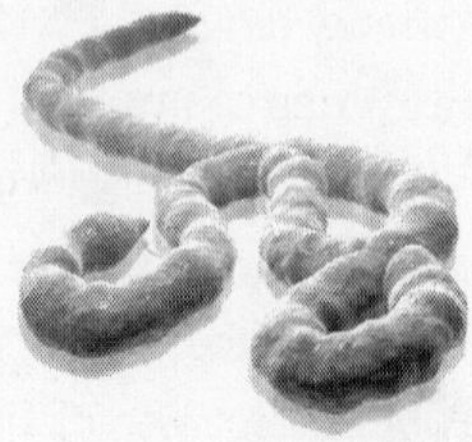

## The most dangerous animal in the world is the common housefly

We cannot avoid the housefly. It is everywhere and is the cause of many common diseases, such as typhoid, diarrhoea, dysentery, cholera. They visit animal waste and transmit more diseases than any other animal through the food we eat.

## When a flea jumps, the rate of acceleration is 20 times that of the space shuttle during launch

The fleas have been found to jump at speeds of 1.9 metres per second catapulting them to a height 50 to 100 times their body length. Using high speed recording technology, scientists discovered that the fleas used the toes to jump and continue accelerating.

## India leads the world in banana production

Bananas are eaten both raw (ripe) and cooked. They are a rich source of many vitamins and potassium. India is the leading producer of bananas with an annual output of about 16.8 metric tons. This means about 23 per cent of the world's total production happens in India.

## Human tapeworms can grow up to 22.9 metres

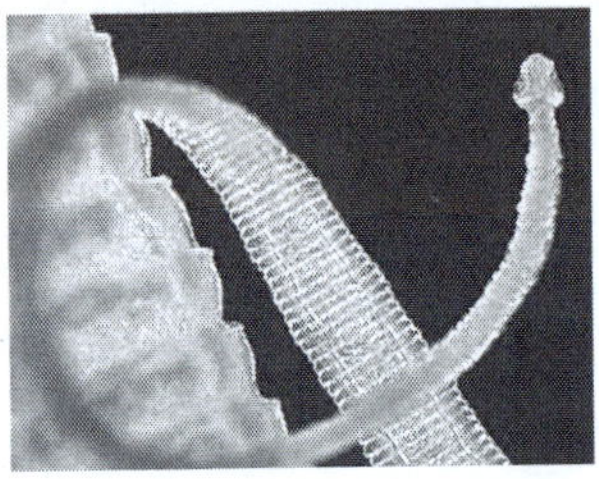

Among the parasites that live in the intestines of humans and animals, the tapeworm is one of the largest and longest. These enter the body through undercooked food. The tapeworms in the intestines of humans can grow very long.

## The thermometer was invented in 1607 by Galileo

In about 1607, Galileo invented an instrument that could measure the rise of water in a glass tube with the rise in temperature. This instrument is called a thermoscope. Later, scientists modified it to add a scale to mark the rise of water. Subsequently, water was replaced with alcohol and mercury.

## An ostrich's eye is bigger than its brain

The ostrich has a very small brain. In proportion to their bodies too, they have smaller brains. It is smaller than its eye, which measures about 5 cm. Ostriches have the largest eyes among the land animals.

## The water that falls on a single acre of land during one inch of rainfall weighs 113 tons

Water falls on earth in form of precipitation, such as snow or rain. Rainfall is the main form of precipitation. The amount of rainfall may vary from region to region. It could be 0.1 inch per year in deserts and 900 inches per year in the tropics. If a one inch rainfall occurred in one acre of land, it would weigh 113 tons.

## The walled city of Delhi originally had fourteen gates

The gates of Delhi were built by different rulers at different times. Delhi is an aggregate of nine cities. In the seventh city built by Shah Jahan, there were 14 gates. However, there are only five gates that are standing today. These are Ajmeri Gate facing Ajmer in Rajasthan; Lahori Gate facing Lahore in Pakistan; Kashmiri Gate pointing North to Kashmir; Delhi Gate with road leading to earlier cities of Delhi and Turkman Gate named after saint Hazrat Shah Turkman.

## Every year, over one million earthquakes shake the earth

The earth is divided into three layers; the upper crust, the middle mantle and the innermost core. The upper crust is made of solid plates, called tectonic plates. Some plates are under the ocean too. The mantle is semi solid and the tectonic plates slide over the mantle, causing an earthquake.

## Elephants have the longest gestation period in the animal kingdom

The elephant has the longest gestation period at 22 months. This is longer than that of the blue whale, which is one year. Some species of dolphins have a gestation period of 17 months and sperm whales carry their young for up to 19 months. Rhinos have a gestation period of about 450 days. Owing to such long gestation, the population of these species are not quickly replenished.

## The eyes of giant squids are the largest on the planet

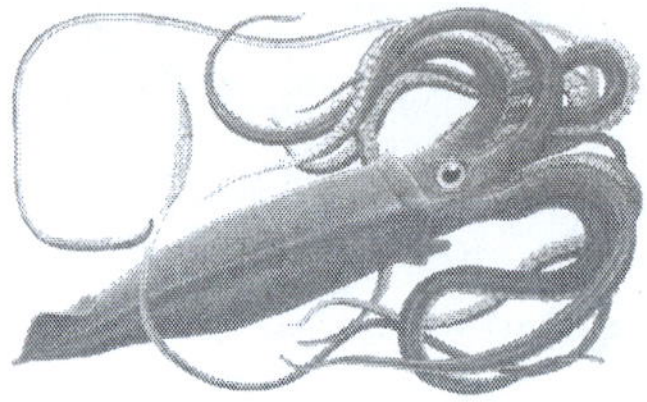

The giant squid (*Architeuthis sp.)* is found in the seas and can grow up to 18 metres in length and weigh up to 900 kg. At 15 inches, that is about 38 cm its eyes are the size of a basketball; the largest eyes on Earth.

## The coldest seas are at the poles

The coldest seas are found near the poles. The Greenland, Barents, Beaufort, Kara, Laptev and East Siberian Seas are found near the north pole. The Weddell and Ross Seas are found in the south pole. The Baltic Sea is also considered one of the coldest seas, but it is not located near the poles.

## The first synthetic human chromosome was constructed by US scientists in 1997

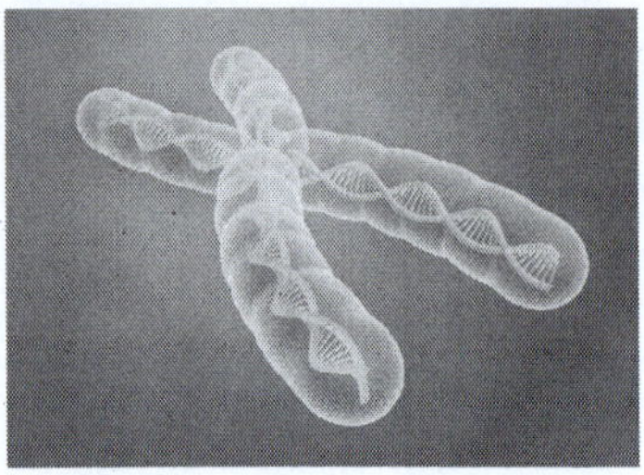

Chromosomes are considered the basic structures of heredity. They carry the codes that give rise to the expression of the characteristic features of an organism. Humans have 46 chromosomes. In 1997, a team of scientists J.J. Harrington, G.V. Bokkelen, R.W. Mays, K. Gustashaw, and H.F. Willard synthesized artificial chromosomes. These chromosomes are stable up to six weeks. These chromosomes can be used as vectors to carry genes of interest into other cells and study of their expression.

## On average, our bodies constantly resist an atmospheric pressure of about 1 kilogram per square cm

The atmosphere surrounding us is made of air. The air molecules have weight and therefore exert pressure on us. This pressure is called atmospheric pressure. The atmospheric pressure has been estimated to be about 1 kg per square cm. This means the pressure on 1000 square cm (about a square foot) is a tons. Our bodies are able to resist this enormous atmospheric pressure because the air pressure inside our bodies is naturally balanced to the external pressure.

## More movies are produced in India than in Hollywood

About 1,000 movies are released in India per year, most of which are produced in Mumbai (called Bollywood). Other regional movies are also produced in almost all major states of India. Hollywood makes about 600 movies per year.

## The Nile River in Africa is the longest river (6,825 kilometres) on the earth

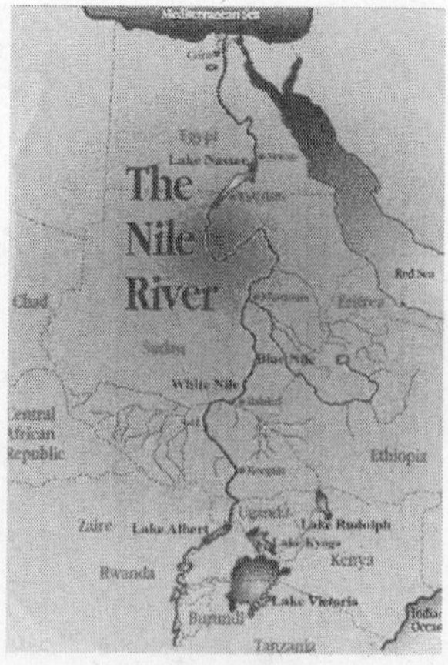


The Nile is one of the most interesting rivers of the world owing to the ancient Egyptian civilization, which is known as the 'Gift of Nile'. The river originates in the well watered regions of North East Africa and proceeds to drain northwards in the Mediterranean Sea. It is the world's longest river measuring 6,825 kilometres.

## On the day that Alexander Graham Bell was buried the entire US telephone system was shut down for 1 minute in tribute

Alexander Graham Bell died on August 4, 1922 and on that day millions of phones in America and Canada went dead for one minute as a mark of respect for the inventor.

## Chandragupta Maurya was guarded by a band of women

Chandragupta Maurya (340 to 290 B.C.) was an eminent king of the Gupta dynasty in India who established the Mauryan Empire from 321 to 185 B.C. Chandragupta is considered the first unifier of India and its first genuine emperor. He was guarded by a band of women on horseback.

## The low frequency call of the humpback whale is the loudest noise made by a living creature

The call made by a humpback whale is of a low frequency and very loud. It is believed to be louder than the Concord. The sound made by the whale can be heard about 805 kilometres away.

## Giraffes often sleep for only 20 minutes in 24 hours

Giraffes need less sleep than any other animal. They may sleep between ten minutes to two hours in 24 hours to regain their energy. They never lie down to sleep.

## Wounds infested with maggots heal quickly and without spread of gangrene or other infection

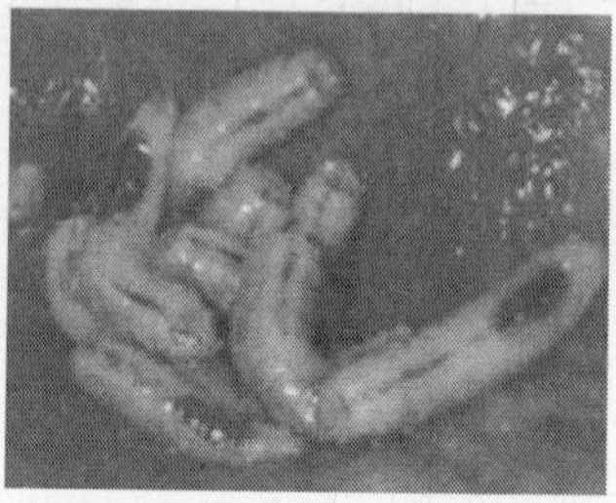

Maggot therapy is used to heal wounds. In this method, the maggot or larvae of flies are allowed to eat away the dead tissue in the wound, thereby clearing it quickly and healing it in the process. It is also known as Maggot Debridement Therapy (MDT).

## There are 60,000 miles (96,560 km) of blood vessels in the body of a child

There are three types of blood vessels in the human body. These are the arteries, vessels and the capillaries. If a child's blood vessels are joined end to end, they would measure 96,560.64 km (60,000 miles), or they could encircle the earth two and a half times. The average adult's blood vessels measure 1,60,934.4 km (1,00,000 miles).

## The Universe contains over 100 billion galaxies

It is estimated that the Universe has 100 billion galaxies. Each galaxy could have billions of stars. The Hubble telescope has enabled us to see the never before seen galaxies in this Universe.

## Peanuts are one of the ingredients of dynamite

The nitroglycerine used in dynamite is derived from glycerol, which could be produced from peanuts. Peanuts are not used directly.

## Every hour the Universe expands by a billion miles in all directions

Edwin Hubble, working on the light emitted by stars found that there was a shift in the light coming from the stars. This means that the stars and galaxies were moving away from each other. This in turn means that the Universe was and is still expanding.

## An individual blood cell takes about 60 seconds to make a complete circuit of the body

The red blood cells continuously flow in the blood vessels of the body via the bloodstream. The speed of the blood cells is fastest at the heart (left ventricle) and slowest at the capillary ends. The time taken by a blood cell to leave the heart, flow through the body and return to the heart, completing a full cycle of circulation, has been estimated at an average value of 60 seconds.

## Somewhere in the flicker of a badly tuned TV set is the background radiation from the Big Bang

When the Universe was formed, the Big Bang resulted in the formation of matter and radiation. This radiation, also called the cosmic microwave background forms the dark body in space. This radiation can be detected in TV screens in between channels as static.

## Isaac Newton (1642), Pandit Madan Mohan Malaviya (1861), Humphrey Bogart (1899), Anwar Sadat (1918), and Marcus Trescothick (1975) were all born on 25th December

Isaac Newton was an English physicist, mathematician and astronomer who discovered gravitation and the three laws of motion. Pandit Madan Mohan Malaviya was a national leader and freedom fighter of India who was a great educationist too; he founded the Banaras Hindu University. Humphrey Bogart was an American actor who was regarded as a cultural icon. Anwar Sadat was the third Egyptian President and was awarded the Nobel Prize for Peace in 1978. Marcus Trescothick is an English cricketer who plays first class cricket. All were born on December 25th.

## Each person sheds 18 kilograms of skin in his or her lifetime

Our skin is made of many layers of cells. The outer layer is flaky and the inner layers have structure giving and nourishing elements. The outer skin gets dry, or damaged with time and so it sheds. An average person sheds about 30,000 cells every minute. Most household dust is made of dead skin.

## Babies are born without fully formed knee caps

Babies are born with kneecaps, but these are not fully formed. They are made of softer tissue, such as cartilage. The cartilages turn into bone after the child reaches 2-6 years of age.

## The most offspring produced by any animal is by a female oyster

A female oyster produces 100 million young in her lifetime. A typical hen lays 19 dozen eggs a year, and one female cat could be responsible for the birth of 50 kittens in four years.

## The fastest speed with which a falling raindrop can hit you is 9 metres per second

A raindrop falls on the earth with varying speeds depending upon its size and weight. The gravity acts on the falling raindrop and the drop picks up speed. But due to air resistance, which is generally proportional to the velocity, the raindrops attain a terminal speed. A larger raindrop would fall much faster at 9 metres per second whereas a smaller raindrop will fall at a much slower speed of 2 metres per second.

## The human brain is about 75 per cent water

The brain is made up of 100 billion neuron cells, which are composed of 75 per cent water. It becomes necessary to drink lots of water to keep the brain functioning efficiently.

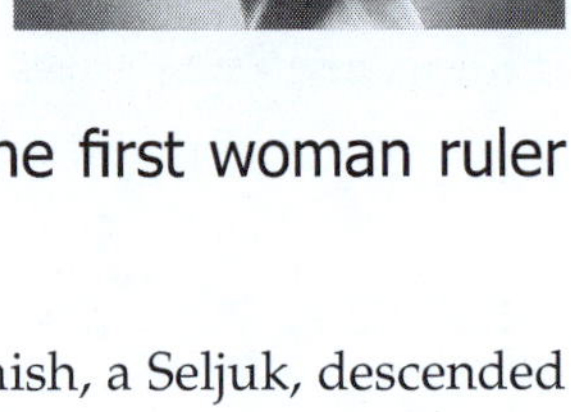

## Razia Sultana (1205–1240) was the first woman ruler of India

Razia Sultana was the daughter of Iltutmish, a Seljuk, descended from the Turkman tribe who ruled India. Born in 1205, Razia was trained to be a ruler by her father. She was considered a great ruler, though she ruled for only three years before being murdered.

## The full name of Los Angeles is 'El Pueblo de Nuestra Señora la Reina de los Angeles de Porciúncula'

In 1769, a Franciscan priest Father Juan Crespí, accompanying the first European land expedition through California described in his journal a "beautiful river from the northwest". He named it *Nuestra Señora de los Angeles de la Porciúncula*. Soon a settlement by the river was established. This settlement was named El Pueblo de Nuestra Señora la Reina de los Angeles de Porciúncula or The Town of Our Lady the Queen of Angels of the Little Portion. The official name was simply *El Pueblo de la Reina de Los Angeles*. The full name can be abbreviated to 3.63 per cent of its original size: 'L.A.'

## Even travelling at the speed of light it would take 2 million years to reach the nearest large galaxy, Andromeda

The Andromeda is a galaxy that is about 2.5 million light years from the Milky Way. To travel in space, we need to achieve the speed of light, which is about 3,00,000 kilometres per second. Even at that great speed, it will take us about 2 million years to reach Andromeda, one of the closest galaxies.

## Possums have one of the shortest gestation periods at 13 days

The lowest gestation period of 12 to 13 days has been found in the marsupials; the American opossum, the water opossum and the eastern native cat. Just like kangaroos, they carry the newborns in a pouch.

## It would take over an hour for a heavy object to sink 6.7 miles (10.7 km) down to the deepest part of the ocean

The average depth of an ocean is 4.3 kilometres. The deepest part of the ocean is the Challenger Deep in the Mariana Trench of the Pacific Ocean. It is estimated that a heavy object will take an hour to sink into Challenger Deep.

## Butterflies cannot fly if their body temperature is less than 86 degrees Fahrenheit

Butterflies are delicate creatures and they are affected by climate changes. A large population of butterflies indicates a healthy ecosystem and a dearth of butterflies indicates that the ecosystem is under stress. They are unable to fly if their body temperatures drop below 86 degrees Fahrenheit.

## The brain consumes 25 watts of power

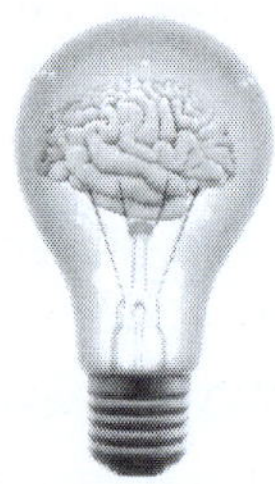

While we are awake, our brain consumes 25 watts of power. This amount of energy is enough to illuminate a lightbulb.

## The national flag of Paraguay has different emblems on the obverse and reverse sides

The flag has an emblem on the obverse side, which is the national coat of arms of Paraguay that comprises a yellow five-pointed star surrounded by a green wreath capped by the words *REPUBLICA DEL PARAGUAY*. The emblem on the reverse side is the seal of the treasury, which is a yellow lion below a red Phrygian cap and the words *PAZ Y JUSTICIA* ('Peace and Justice').

## Every minute 750 ml of blood get pumped through your brain, which is 15–20 per cent of blood flow from the heart

An adult brain requires about 20 per cent of the body's oxygen. To meet this requirement, and other metabolic needs of the neurons, approximately 20 per cent of the blood flow is directed to the brain.

## Wearing headphones for just an hour will increase the bacteria in your ear by ten times

Scientists in India carried out a study on students using earphones. They found that frequent use and sharing of earphones increase the bacterial growth in external ear.

## Case Moth caterpillars build a case around themselves that they always carry with them

Case Moth caterpillars (Psychidae) make a case around them, which is made of silk and pieces of plants or soil. They complete their entire life cycle in the case. When they grow old they shrivel up and fall off the case. Their progenies are born in the case.

## Neurons multiply at a rate of 2,50,000 per minute during early pregnancy

An average adult brain weighs between 1,300 to 1,400 grams. During the development of the foetus, in early pregnancy, about 2,50,000 brain cells or neurons are developed per minute in the foetus.

## The electric chair was invented by a dentist

Till recently, criminals in the US were executed using an electric chair. Nowadays the more humane form of execution by lethal injection is practised. Before the electric chair, the condemned criminals were hanged. However, a dentist Dr. Alfred P. Southwick happened to witness a drunken man getting electrocuted and dying instantly when he touched a live electric generator. He was horrified. However, it later occurred to him that this method of electrocution could be used to humanely execute condemned criminals. As a dentist he worked using chairs, so the idea of the instrument occurred in the form of a chair.

## Three American Presidents died on the fourth of July

The fourth of July is celebrated as the Independence Day in the US. Coincidentally, three US Presidents died on the fourth of July. They were John Adams and Thomas Jefferson, who died on the same day in 1826, and James Monroe, who died in 1831.

## Flies jump backwards during takeoff

Researchers found out using a high speed video camera that the fruitfly anticipates the direction of the threat and shuffles its legs to a takeoff position in a matter of a few milliseconds, a maneuver that helps them fly away from the threat.

## Termites outweigh humans by almost ten to one

There are more termites than humans on this earth. According to scientists the total weight of the termites on earth is ten times that of the total weight of humans. A termite hill sometimes measures more than 10 metres in height making it the tallest structures built by insects.

## Fish that live more than 800 metres below the ocean surface don't have eyes

Sunlight does not reach the depths of the ocean. At the depths of 800 metres below the ocean surface, the creatures have adapted to the dark conditions. They do not have eyes and use their senses to detect pressure and temperature.

## Charles Darwin predicted the existence of a bizarre moth with nearly a foot long proboscis

In 1862, Charles Darwin discovered an orchid from Madagascar with a one foot long spur that held the pollen and the nectar at its depths. He predicted that there must be an insect that had a foot long tongue (proboscis) to pollinate the plant. Nobody had seen such a moth and the idea was laughed at. In 1903, the Morgan's Sphinx Moth was discovered that has a proboscis 12 to 14 inches long to get the nectar from the bottom of the 12 inch deep orchid spur.

## Butterflies range in size from a tiny 1/8 inch to a huge almost 12 inches

The size of the butterfly depends on the wingspan and the body. The butterfly with the biggest wingspan is the Queen Alexandra's Birdwing, which has a wingspan up to 1 feet (30 cm) wide.

## Luna moths never eat anything as adults because they don't have mouths

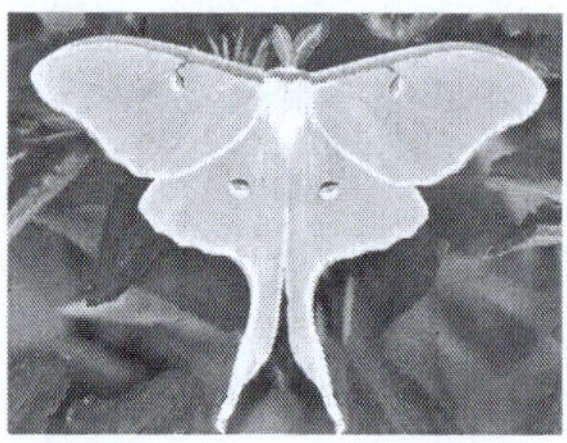

There are several types of moths like the Luna moths, which do not have a mouth. They live on the energy they stored as caterpillars. These moths live for only a week and die after mating.

## The easiest colour to spot is yellow

Researchers had found that the human eye spots the colour yellow very fast. Following this cue, John Herz, founder of the Yellow Cab company, picked up the yellow colour for cabs so that they would be easy to locate by travellers.

## One in eight million people has progeria, a disease that causes people to grow faster than they age

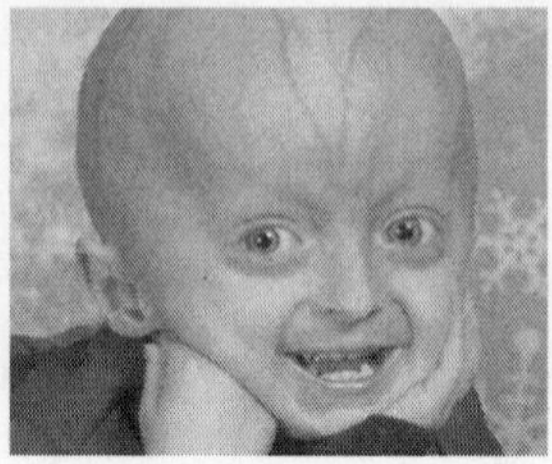

Progeria is derived from the Greek words *pro* meaning before and *geria* meaning old age. It is technically called the Hutchinson-Gilford Progeria Syndrome. It is a disease that causes a person to age faster than the norm. People with progeria do not survive beyond their teens.

## The male sea horse carries the eggs until they hatch instead of the female

The male sea horse has a pouch at its front. During mating, the female sea horse deposits about 1,500 eggs in this pouch. The male sea horse incubates the eggs until they are hatched.

## In 10 minutes a hurricane releases more energy than all of the world's nuclear weapons combined

An average hurricane bringing in 1.5 cm per day of rain, with a circle radius of 665 km generates a huge amount of energy ($6.0 \times 10^{14}$ Watts or $5.2 \times 10^{19}$ Joules/day), which is equivalent of 200 times the electricity generating capacity of the entire planet in a year. This is equivalent to detonating a ten megaton nuclear bomb every 20 minutes.

## The glue on Israeli postage is certified *kosher*

*Kosher* is a Hebrew word that means 'fit or proper' as a dietary material. The glue in the postage stamps in Israel is made of an edible material because stamps are almost always licked for pasting on to the envelope.

## Negative emotions such as anxiety and depression can weaken your immune system

Anxiety and depression can lower the resistance to diseases by weakening the immune system. Negative thoughts increase anxiety and depression. Positive thoughts could reduce these symptoms.

## Giraffes and kangaroo rats can live longer without water than camels

Camels are known to live without water for many weeks in the desert. But it has been found that giraffes and kangaroo rats can live for more days than the camels. The giraffes eat food high in water content and so they can live without water for weeks. The kangaroo rats never drink water but metabolise water from the seeds they eat.

## Mercury is the only planet whose orbit is coplanar with its equator

Mercury is the first planet from the sun and is about the size of the earth's moon. The axis of Mercury has a very small tilt and its orbit is coplanar with its equator.

## US Dollar bills are made out of cotton and linen

The Dollar bills are made of a special kind of paper called the rag. It contains wood pulp, cotton, silk and linen. The rag also contains red and blue synthetic fibres that are distributed evenly.

## Many people eat insects

The practice of people eating insects is called Entomophagy (people eating bugs). It has been practiced for centuries throughout Africa, Australia, Asia, the Middle East, and North, Central and South America. This is because many bugs are both protein-rich and good sources of vitamins, minerals and fats.

## Every person, including identical twins, has a unique eye and tongue print along with their finger print

Tongue prints are as distinctive as eye and finger prints. The technique of biometry is being used to identify individuals using the uniqueness of the iris of an individual. Nowadays, tongue prints are also being considered for biometrics, since tongues are protected in the mouth and hence difficult to forge.

## In Italy, 17 is considered an unlucky number

The number 17 can be written in Roman as XVII. When these numerals are rearranged it reads VIXI, which means in Latin 'I have lived', meaning 'my life is over'. The number 17 is therefore considered unlucky in Italy.

## Camels have three eyelids

Camels have upper and lower eyelids that have eyelashes to shield the eyes from sand. In addition, the camels have a third eyelid, which is thin like a transparent membrane. It opens sideways, from both sides, like a shutter. Camels can see through this third eyelid during sandstorms.

## Paraskevidekatriaphobia means fear of Friday the $13^{th}$

The term Paraskevidekatriaphobia was coined by the Russian doctor Dr. Donald Dossey to denote the fear of Friday the $13^{th}$, which is known as Friggatriskaidecaphobia. Frigga was a Roman goddess of fertility whose day was Friday. Many people have a morbid fear of Friday the $13^{th}$, which occurs one to three times a year.

## Fungi are more closely related to human beings and animals than to other plants

Researchers have come to the conclusion that fungi are closer to animals and humans than to plants. Earlier it was believed that fungi were close to plants. This finding is based on the genetic data obtained recently. Accordingly the fungi have been designated a separated kingdom along with the plant kingdom and animal kingdom.

## There are bananas called 'Red banana' that are maroon to dark purple when ripe

The red bananas mostly grow in Asia and South America. The skin of these bananas turn red to purple. The flesh is usually light pink and tastes slightly like raspberries. These are highly relished all over the world.

## In Japan, 4 is considered an unlucky number

The number 4 is pronounced as 'shi' in Japanese, which means death. So the Japanese consider 4 as an unlucky number. None of the hospitals have 4 as a room number. There are no floors marked 4 in the hotels and highrises.

## Black pepper is the most popular spice in the world

Black pepper accounts for about 20 per cent of the spices traded in the world, making it the most popular among spices. It is pungent and versatile that allows it to be added to any food. It is known to improve digestion.

## Almonds and peaches are members of the rose family

Almond plants belong to the same family as the rose (*Rosaceae*). The other plants that belong to the rose family are plum, cherry, apricot and peach.

## Corals grow one centimetre in one year

Corals are small colourful marine animals that are found in the seas. They build the coral reefs. Their exoskeletons provide the structure of the reefs. The reefs are of high ecological importance. Corals grow very slowly at the rate of about one centimetre a year.

## Every human spent about half an hour as a single cell

During fertilization of the egg by the sperm, the DNA of the sperm is injected into the egg. Both the sperm and the egg have a single set of chromosomes, but the fertilized egg receives the DNA from the sperm and comes to possess both the sets of chromosomes. This fertilized egg cell stays as such for about half an hour and then proceeds to divide to form the multicellular embryo. Thus, all of us have spent about half an hour as a single cell.

## Chocolate can kill dogs

Chocolate contains a chemical called theobromine. It is toxic to dogs at doses of 100 to 150 milligrams per body weight. The high doses of the chemical directly affects the dog's heart and nervous system.

## There are no two zebras which have stripes that are exactly the same

All zebras have black and white stripes, but they differ in their pattern. In fact, no two zebras have the same pattern. It is believed that the patterns can confuse a predator like a lion, when the zebras are in a herd, making it difficult to separate and kill a zebra.

## Most lipstick contains fish scales

Lipsticks use an ingredient called pearl essence to impart shimmer to the lips. This ingredient is harvested from the herring, a fish that has shimmering scales. Herring fish scales are also used in nail polish.

## The Basenji dog is the only dog that is not able to bark

The Basenji dogs cannot bark because their larynx is unusually shaped. However, they are not mute. They produce a unique sound resembling a 'yodel' or a howl. Some may whine and 'scream' as protest.

## Ketchup was sold in the 1830s as medicine

In the US, till the 1800, tomato was considered to be poisonous. But in 1830s it became very popular. It was sold under the name of 'Dr. Miles' Compound Extract of Tomato, and claimed to cure many ailments.

## Goats do not have upper front teeth

Goats have gum in place of their upper front teeth, called a dental pad. However they have very strong molars at the back of the mouth. They have full set of lower teeth. Cows, antelopes and other ruminants also do not have front incisors.

## Tomatoes and cucumbers are fruits

Botanically, a fruit is derived from the parts of a flower. A fruit contains seeds. When we look at a tomato or a cucumber, we find that they have seeds. So, technically tomatoes and cucumbers are fruits, not vegetables.

## There is cyanide in apple seeds

Cyanide is a lethal chemical, which is found in minute amounts in some seeds, such as apple and mango. If you accidentally swallow an apple seed or two, you'll be fine, but if you eat enough apple seeds, you could die.

## Odontophobia is the fear of teeth care

The irrational fear against dental care is called odontophobia. *Odonto* means teeth and *phobia* means fear in Greek. Odontophobia mostly results from previous traumatic experience with teeth removal or similar dentist care.

## A crocodile cannot stick its tongue out

The tongue of a crocodile is connected to the lower part of its mouth by a thin membrane. So, it cannot stick its tongue out. Interestingly, the crocodile's tongue functions the same way as our kidneys, that is to filter out salts.

## Albert Einstein and Charles Darwin both married their first cousins

Albert Einstein married his first cousin Elsa Löwenthal after divorcing his first wife. He and Elsa didn't have any children. Charles Darwin married his first cousin Emma Wedgwood and they had ten children.

## The Kodiak is the world's largest bear

The Kodiak (*Ursus arctos middendorffi*) is found in Alaska. It is the largest species of brown bear. The male bear can measure up to eight feet, that is about 2.5 m and weigh as much as 773 kilograms. The female bear is 20 per cent smaller and weighs 30 per cent less than males.

## Mosquito repellents don't repel

Mosquito repellents are made from chemical ingredients, such as pyrethrin. The spray or repellent containing these chemicals blocks the mosquito's sensors so they don't know you're there. Since they cannot detect you, they cannot bite you.

## Mawlynnong is the cleanest village in Asia

Mawlynnong is located in Meghalaya, about 90 kilometres from Shillong. It is nestled in the East Khasi hills where the villagers have learnt to live in harmony with nature. In 2005, the Discover India Magazine accorded it the status of the cleanest village in Asia.

## Adobe is named after a stream

Adobe is a famous software company that develops software like Flash and pdf. The founder John Warnock had a stream behind his house called Adobe. He named the company after this stream.

## Switching letters is called spoonerism

Spoonerism is a disorder in speech where the vowels and consonants are unintentionally or intentionally switched. Spoonerism was named after Reverend William Spooner who had this impediment. One example of Spoonerism is, 'The weight of rages will press hard upon the employer' instead of 'rate of wages', is a spoonerism. Other examples include 'A blushing crow' (A crushing blow); 'A well-boiled icicle' (A well-oiled bicycle), and 'A lack of pies' (A pack of lies).

## Sharp got its name from pencils

The company Sharp that manufactures electronic goods today, used to manufacture pencils. The company was named Sharp after the ever-sharp pencils.

## Parrotfish can make themselves a sleeping bag

The parrotfish is found in the deep seas. During night it covers itself in a gelatinous substance. This substance is produced by the fish from its mucus from the glands located at the upper edge of its gill cavity. This forms a protective sheath and other fishes of prey cannot smell them out at night.

## Men's shirts have the buttons on the right while women's shirts have the buttons on the left

It seems that in the nineteenth century men's fashion was inspired by military use and women's fashion by domestic use. In those times, rich men dressed themselves while the rich women were dressed by servants. Men's jackets had buttons on the right to enable the majority of right handed men to open the buttons easily. When used in armours, it disabled the opponents to jam a sword through the seam. The right handed servants of the women found it easy to help the lady with dressing. It is also believed that the left side buttons helped the women to nurse their babies easily.

## The UK stamps are the only stamps in the world that do not bear the name of the country

The first country to issue postage stamps in the world was Great Britain. It issued the stamps on 1 May, 1840. Hence, UK stamps do not bear the name of the country of origin.

## Soap was first used in 2500 B.C.

The use of soap dates back to about 5,000 years. The ancient Sumerians used a soap made of water, alkali and cassia oil. This soap was perhaps used for washing clothes, especially wool, and not for personal hygiene.

## No word in the English language rhymes with month, silver or purple

A rhyme is a word that repeats the sound of another word. For example, 'fill' rhymes with uphill, bill; 'today' rhymes with play, clay, etc. However, there are three English words that do not rhyme with any word and these are 'month', 'silver' and 'purple'.

## *Chandamama* is the longest running children's magazine in India

*Chandamama* was launched in July 1947 by Chakrapani in Telugu. It is published in 13 languages including English. It is also published in Santhali, making it the only children's magazine in Santhali.

## The Anna's Hummingbird is the fastest animal on earth

A hummingbird flaps its wings up to 90 times in one second or over 5,000 times a minute. The Anna's Hummingbird can pull up or dive during courtship at amazing speeds. When pulling up, it experiences forces that are ten times that of gravity. While diving down, it flies at the speed of 93 kilometres per hour.

## The word 'fortnight' is a contraction of 'fourteen nights'

A fortnight means fourteen days. It is derived from the old English word fēowertyne niht, meaning '14 nights'. In the US 'two weeks' is more commonly used instead of a fortnight.

## In a statue of a person on a horse, the position of the legs of the horse indicate how the person riding it died

If a statue of a person on a horse has both front legs in the air, the person died in battle; if the horse has one front leg in the air, the person died as a result of wounds received in battle; if the horse has all four legs on the ground, the person died of natural cause.

## The pink diamond is the world's rarest and most valuable diamond

The Argyle mine at East Kimberley, Western Australia, yields the world's most exquisite shades of pink diamonds. The diamonds have been sold for up to one million dollars a carat.

## Elvis Presley worked for a truck company

Elvis Presley, the cultural icon of the 70s, worked for a truck company as a driver before he was discovered. The trucking company where Elvis Presley worked as a young man was owned by Frank Sinatra.

## Fifty new earth-like planets have been found beyond the solar system

Scientists and astronomers in Europe discovered 50 new planets and believe at least 16 planets have water, and have a life on them. Some of these planets have the same mass as Earth, while others are such as 10 times heavier. Astronomers believe that the development of life on them was feasible and easier than on our planet Earth.

## The youngest author of a book was only four years old

Dorothy Straight of Washington, D.C., was only 4 years old in 1962 when she wrote *How the World Began* for her grandmother. Her parents sent it to a publisher and the book was published in 1964, two years later.

## More than 9,700 languages and dialects are spoken in the world

There are about 2,700 languages and more than 7,000 dialects. A dialect is a regional variety of a language that has a different pronunciation, vocabulary, or meaning. A language has a script but a dialect does not. India is home to 1,650 languages and dialects.

## Dinosaur means 'frightful lizard'

The name dinosaur was coined by the British naturalist Sir Richard Owen. He found the prehistoric monster to be a frightful creature and named it dinosaur. The name is derived from two Greek words, *deinos* meaning frightful and *sauros* meaning lizard.

## The people in Bali only have one of four names: Wayan, Made, Nyoman, and Ketut

The Balinese people only have four first names. The first child is named Wayan, the second child is Made, the third is Nyoman and the fourth is Ketut. The fifth, sixth, seventh, eighth and ninth will be again named Wayan, Made, Nyoman, Ketut and Wayan again.

## The attachment of the human skin to muscles is what causes dimples

Dimples are small indentations on the cheeks. Dimples could be observed when a person is smiling. These are formed because a muscle in the face – zygomaticus major – is shorter than normal and pulls down the overlying skin when stretched, thus causing a dimple.

## Candy got its name from the Sanskrit word *khanda*

The confection candy is derived from the Italian word candi, which in turn is derived from the Sanskrit word *khanda* meaning pieces of something.

## The name of fruit 'date' means finger

The ancient people thought that the fruit of the date palm resembled the human finger. So they named it *dactylus,* which is a Latin word meaning 'finger'.

## Radio waves can be heard sooner at a distance than at the place where it originates

Radio waves travel at 2,99,338 kilometres per second and sound waves move at 1,127 kilometres per hour, a broadcast voice can be heard sooner 20,000 kilometres away than it can be heard at the back of the room in which it originated.

## The word 'Bungalow' originated from Bengal

The name 'Bungalow' gained prominence in India during the British times in the 17$^{th}$ century. It is derived from the word 'Bangla', which means 'Of Bengal' in Bengali. Bungalows are generally one and a half storey houses with a front porch. The architecture is typical of East India houses.

## 'Mayday' means 'help me' in French

The word 'Mayday' comes from the French word *m'aidez* – meaning 'help me'. Ships and aircrafts use this word when in distress as their call for help.

## Duck is named so because it dives in water

When the duck swims, it occasionally dives in the water to catch fish or insects. Its name is derived from this diving action.

## Rounded table knives were designed by a French nobleman

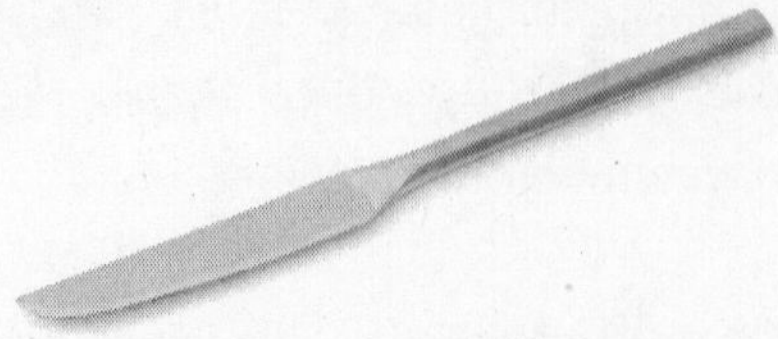

Originally, the table knives were pointed. One day Duc de Richelieu, a French nobleman saw one of his guests pick his teeth with a knife. The next day he ordered that all knives be made blunt having rounded ends.

## Tulip means Turban

Tulip is a beautiful flower with velvety petals and fascinating colours. Its name is derived from the French word *tulipan,* which in turn is derived from the Turkish word *tulbend,* meaning turban.

## The word bribe means 'a piece of bread'

Bribe is a French word which originally meant a piece of bread given to a beggar. Today the word has come to mean a sum of money given to someone to persuade.

## The word candidate means 'clad in white'

During the Roman times, a person used to dress in white to create a good impression among others. The Latin word *candidatus* was used to describe a person dressed in white. The word candidate is derived from *candidatus.*

## The term fascism means 'based on a bundle of sticks'

The word fascism is derived from the Italian word *fascismo,* which in turn is derived from the Latin word *fascis,* which means a bundle, usually of sticks or rods.

## Curfew means 'to cover the fire'

In the middle ages in Europe, there was a law that householders should extinguish the fires after a bell was rung in the evening. The word curfew is derived from the French word *couvre feu*, which means to 'cover fire'.

## Amoeba means 'change'

The amoeba is a microscopic aquatic animal, which constantly changes its shape. Its name is derived from the Greek word *amoibe*, which means change.

## Scottish kings lived in Scotland Yard

The Scotland Yard is very famous in the detective stories. This place was a palace where the kings of Scotland used to stay when they visited England.

## Papples are a new fruit that look like apples and taste like pears

Papples are a hybrid between two European and Asian pear varieties that look like apples. These have been developed in New Zealand, where they are officially known as PremP109.

## In British Guiana men and women speak two different languages

The men of British Guiana speak Arawak. The women are not allowed to speak Arawak. They speak another language called Carib.

## Beethoven disliked the name 'Moonlight sonata' for his famous composition

When the music critic Rellstab heard the Beethoven's popular work Op. 27, No. 2, he was reminded of moonlight on Lake Lucerne and called the piece 'Moonlight Sonata'. The name displeased Beethoven, but the name became popular.

## Senate means a group of old men

The word senate is derived from the Latin word *senates* meaning old men or a revered men or council of elders.

## 'Day' means 'to burn'

The word 'day' is derived from the Sanskrit word *dah*, which means 'to burn'. The word *dah* became the old English word dæg and later became 'day'.

## The Mona Lisa used to hang on the wall of Napoleon's bedroom

The famous painting Mona Lisa by Leonardo da Vinci was in the possession of Napoleon briefly after the French Revolution in his Tuileries Palace. He hung the painting in his bedroom.

## Arable means 'the land that can be ploughed'

The word arable is used to designate the parts of land that could be ploughed or dug for cultivation purposes. It is derived from the Latin word *arable*, which means 'that can be ploughed'.

## Rubber bands last longer when refrigerated

Rubber is made of polymers, molecules that have the same basic structure that are repeated over and over. When it is heated, the molecules become disordered and chances of the rubber breaking become more. On cooling, the molecules become ordered and chances of breaking become low.

## Cereal for breakfast was invented by John Henry Kellogg

John Henry Kellogg was a physician who worked to develop a healthy diet. Kellogg and his brother, Will Keith Kellogg, invented several foods made from grains. The foods were rolled and made into sheets of dough, which were cooked. One day they accidentally left the cereals for a longer period of time and these were passed through the rollers to emerge as flakes. They had discovered the cereal flakes.

## The cellphone brand Nokia is named after a place in Southern Finland

Nokia is a place in Finland. It means 'soot marten' in Finnish, which means the sable. Nokia is situated in the banks of the Nokianvirta River. The town has a population of about 32,000 people.

## The opposite sides of a dice always adds up to seven

A dice has 1 opposite 6, 2 opposite 5, and 3 opposite 4. As you can see, these numbers add up to seven.

## Porsche also builds tractors

The history of Porsche tractors can be traced back to 1934 when Ferdinand Porsche produced three prototype tractors, all equipped with petrol engines. Since Porsche was not a farm tractor producing company, after the World War II, it signed licensing agreements with the German company Allgaier GmbH and the Austrian company Hofherr Schrantz to produce the tractors.

## Zero scores in tennis are called 'love', which means egg in French

Tennis was popular in France. The score zero when marked on the scoreboard looked like an egg. This zero was called *l'oeuf,* which is French for 'egg.' When tennis was introduced in the US, Americans began to pronounce it 'love.'

## The Indonesian jungle harbours many unknown species

The Indonesian jungle is home to dozens of hitherto unknown animal and plant species. The Indonesian forests are tropical rainforests that are rich in biodiversity. In February 2006, the BBC reported that an international team of scientists had found a previously unknown jungle in Indonesia containing new species of butterflies, frogs, birds and plants.

## The piggy bank was actually named after pygg, a type of clay

In Europe, kitchen utensils were made of an orange clay called pygg. People used to save their coins in jars made of pygg. An English potter was asked to make such a pygg jar as a bank for storing coins. He misunderstood pygg for pig and shaped the jar like a pig. This was the origin of piggy banks.

## A company in Taiwan makes dinnerware out of wheat, so that you can eat your plate

Edible utensils have been always been there since time immemorial. People used to make plates out of bread called trenchers. Now a company in Taiwan has started manufacturing edible dinnerware, which you can use to serve food in and also eat it.

## To be 'in the limelight' is derived from light derived from lime

To be 'in the limelight' means to be famous. The limelight was invented in 1825, by burning a cylinder of lime (calcium oxide) that produced a brilliant light. This light was used in lighthouses and theatres. In the theatre, a performer was focused with the limelight to make him or her the centre of attention.

## Monsoons are still predicted using the instruments at Jantar Mantar in Jaipur, India

The prediction of monsoons is done using several centuries old instrument known as the *Samrat Yantra* at the Jantar Mantar constructed in 1724 by Maharaja Jai Singh. The prediction is done by observing the wind direction using the 90 feet high *Samrat Yantra* and a 25 feet high flag on top of it that takes the total height to 115 feet. The flow of eastern wind confirms good monsoons.

## A jumbo jet uses 33,390 litres of fuel to take off

A jumbo jet of about 400 tons needs a lot of power to move the plane forward and take off. It uses up about 33,390 litres of fuel just for the take off.

## Bird droppings are the chief export of Nauru, an island nation in the Western Pacific

Nauru is a small country in the Pacific. Covering just 21 square kilometres, it is world's smallest republic. Its economy is dependent solely on the phosphate deposits made by the droppings of sea birds.

## The word 'modem' is a contraction of the words 'modulate and demodulate' (MOdulate DEModulate)

A modem is a device that enables a computer to transmit data over, for example, telephone or cable lines. The word is the acronym derived from **mo**dulator/**dem**odulator.

## Unless food is mixed with saliva you can't taste it

The salivary glands in our mouths form saliva that mix with the food and dissolve the molecules in the food. Unless the molecules are thus dissolved, the taste buds cannot sense the taste of the food.

## The hydrogen molecules in water are as old as the universe

When you drink a glass of water next time think about this: the hydrogen molecules present in the water are 14 billion years old. They were created at the same time as the universe.

## Japanese farmers grow square watermelons

The Japanese farmers have figured out a way to utilize space for watermelons in the refrigerator. While still on the vine, the growing young watermelons are kept in square boxes made of glass. The square boxes are the exact dimensions of Japanese refrigerators.

## The popping sound you hear when you crack your knuckles is actually a bubble of gas bursting

The joints between the bones contain a clear fluid called the synovial fluid. It acts as a lubricant. When we crack the knuckles, the two bones are pulled apart. This results in a gap in the joint and the pressure on the synovial fluid is reduced forming bubbles that quickly burst making the popping noise.

## Cryovolcano is a volcano that shoots up cold liquid

A cryovolcano is found in icy moons. It shoots up cold liquid rather than lava. The cold liquid is a mixture of water, methane or ammonia (called cryomagma). The cold liquid cools and becomes solid as soon as it hits the surface. The Sotra Facula volcano on Titan, the moon of Saturn, is a dormant cryovolcano.

## The liquid inside young coconuts can be used as a substitute for blood plasma

During World War II, when blood plasma supply was low, doctors discovered that the liquid inside coconut can be used as a substitute for blood plasma. It has been found that coconut water is isotonic to blood plasma and does not destroy the blood cells.

## The word 'pound' is abbreviated 'lb' after the constellation 'libra'

The constellation Libra means 'pound' in Latin, and also 'scales'. Libra is abbreviated as lb, which is used to designate the British Pound Sterling. The British currency (before it went metric) was always quoted as 'pounds/shillings/pence', abbreviated 'L.S.D.' (libra/solidus/denarius).

## The word 'sniper' is derived from a bird 'snipe' in India

In the $19^{th}$ century, the British soldiers in India used to test their marksmanship by hunting a bird 'snipe'. The snipe is an elusive bird and whoever hit the bird was called a sniper.

## More than half of the coastline of the entire United States is in Alaska

Alaska has the longest coastline among all the states of the USA. It has a coastline of 10,686 kilometres and the total coastline of USA is about 19,928 km.

## Rats cannot vomit. That is why rat poison works

Rats have a digestion mechanism that does not allow it to vomit up poisonous food. When they ingest lethal amounts of poison, they are not able to throw up and they die.

## Lactose tolerance is due to a mutation in the natural lactose intolerance gene

Most people in the world cannot digest milk. This is called lactose intolerance and is caused due to high level of lactose, a kind of sugar, in the milk. The symptoms of lactose intolerance include nausea and bloating. Lactose intolerance is due to a normal gene. In contrast, lactose tolerance is due to a mutation in the gene.

## Alaska has more than three million lakes

There are more than three million lakes in Alaska larger than 20 acres in size. It has about 3,197 officially named natural lakes.

## The national anthem of the United States of America does not contain the words United States or America

If you read the lyrics of all four stanzas of the American National Anthem 'The Star Spangled Banner,' you'll find that there are three words missing. The words 'United States' and the word 'America' are never mentioned in the song.

## More capital cities begin with 'B' than any other letter

It is interesting to note that more capital cities begin with the letter 'B' than any other letter. These are: Berlin, Bern, Bucharest, Budapest, Buenos Aires, Brasilia, Baghdad, Beirut, Bratislava, Brussels, Belgrade, Bogota and Belfast.

## Secretary means keeper of confidences

Secretary originates from the Latin term *secretarious*, which means 'one who keeps your secrets'.

## A rainbow is seen as an entire circle from the plane

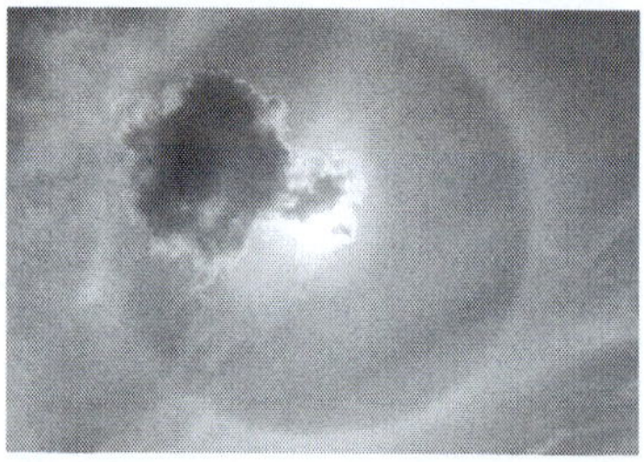

A rainbow is formed just after a rain when the white sunlight is broken into multiple colours by water droplets in the atmosphere. Rainbows that are seen on the earth's surface are usually in the shape of an arc, because the full circle of the rainbow is blocked by the horizon. However, pilots who fly high have reported to have seen circular rainbows.

## The word foetus is Latin for little one

A foetus is a developing baby in the womb. It is very small in size. Referring to its size, the baby is called foetus, which means 'little one' in Latin.

## Heterochromia iridium is a condition where the colour of one eye is different from the other

Heterochromia iridium is a condition where there is a difference in the colour of the eyes. This results due to the difference of the concentration of the pigment melanin in the eyes. This condition is either genetic or occurs due to injury, inflammation, etc. It is frequently found in animals where a blue eye is found in cats or dogs in place of the normal brown or yellow eye.

## Yawning is contagious

Yawning has been found to be contagious. Even thinking about it may bring about a yawn. Research shows that foetuses yawn at 11 weeks. Men yawn longer than women. Animals yawn. There is a 50 per cent chance that after reading this fact, you will yawn.

## Henry Waterman invented the elevator in 1850

Henry Waterman was a resident of New York. He intended to transport barrels of flour up the high-rise buildings. There was a problem with hydraulic lifts that were in operation. He devised the rope and pulley method of the lifts.

## There is an underwater post office in Vanuatu

The world's only underwater post office is located in the Hideaway Island marine sanctuary, in the Republic of Vanuatu. It is in the South Pacific and the post office is 50 metres offshore and just three metres below the waters.

## India has more English speakers than the United Kingdom

There are 232 million English speakers in India. This makes India the second country in the world after the United States (251 million) to have English speaking people. The United Kingdom has about 59 million English speakers.

## The pharaohs of ancient Egypt invented and wore garments made of gold

The fabric was made from thin threads of beaten gold. Some fabrics had up to 500 gold threads per one inch of cloth. In India too, gold threads have been used in clothing since ancient times.

## In ancient Egypt workers received beer as part of their salary

Beer was the staple drink of ancient Egyptians. It was enjoyed by adults and children, the poor and the rich. It was so important that the workers were paid wages in beer.

## Some meteorites are sweet as they are made of a substance similar to sugar

NASA scientists have found sugar and several related substances in meteorites. These meteorites are carbon-rich. It is speculated that meteorites provided such life-building molecules on Earth millions of years ago.

## The most expensive Rolls Royce was named Star of India

The Rolls Royce was built for the Maharaja of Rajkot in 1934. It is now in the possession of a German Rolls Royce collector and is worth US $14,60,000.

## There is an office building in Japan with highway passing through it

The Japanese engineers found an ingenious method to use space when they built the exit of the Hanshin Highway through the Gate Tower building in Fukushima-ku, Osaka. The exit passes through the fifth and seventh floors of the building. The elevators pass through the floors without stopping.

## Scientists have reversed aging in mice

Scientists have partially reversed the aging process in mice using genetic engineering. These mice showed new growth of the brain and testes, improved fertility, and the return of a lost cognitive function.

## The word oxymoron is an oxymoron itself

An oxymoron is a word, which combines contradictory terms. The word 'oxymoron' is derived from the Greek words 'sharp dull'. An oxymoron itself is an oxymoron.

## Fire rainbows are created from ice

The fire rainbows are spectacular phenomenon in the sky. These are formed by plate shaped ice crystals in the clouds high up in the sky. These are also called the circumhorizontal arcs.

## January is named after the Roman God Janus

January is the first month of the year when we bid farewell to the old year and welcome the new. January is named after the Roman God Janus. Janus is represented with two faces. One face is believed to be looking towards the past and the other face towards the future.

## February is named after the Roman Goddess Februaria

In ancient Rome, religious ceremonies were observed in the middle of the second month in which women were beaten for barrenness. In this festival, goats were sacrificed and thongs were made from their skins and given to two selected youths. These youths ran around the city and gave 'curative' slaps to barren women in the city. This month was named after Februaria, the Roman Goddess of fertility.

## March is named after Mars

This month was observed by Romans as the month of spring, and also war. Since the Roman God of war was Mars, this month was named after him.

## April is named after the word 'open'

In ancient Italy, the month of April saw the blooming of the first flowers of the season. The opening of the buds gave the month its name. The Roman word for opening was *Aprilis*.

## May is named after Maia, Mother of the Roman God Hermes

May is Maius in Latin. Maius is believed to be derived from Maia, who was the mother of the God Hermes. May was considered unlucky for marriage.

## June is named after the Roman Goddess Juno

Goddess Juno was considered the protectress of women. June was considered lucky for marriages.

## July is named after Julius Caesar

Mark Anthony proposed that the seventh month of the year may be named Julius in the honour of the birthday of Gaius Julius Caesar. The name however, came to be used in the year of Caesar's assassination. The English named the month Julie before making it July.

## August is named after the Roman Emperor Augustus

The nephew of Julius Caesar, Octavian, wanted to have a name after him, just like his uncle. Octavian was named Augustus by the Senate. Octavian chose the eighth month of the year to be given his name Augustus, which has been shortened to August.

## September is named after the Latin word for seven

The Roman year started in March and so September was their seventh month. The word September was taken from the Latin word *septem,* which meant seven. When the calendar was changed, September became the ninth month, but the name was not changed.

## October is named after the Latin word for eight

The Roman calendar had October as its eighth month. *Octo* in Latin means eight. The name was not changed when the calendar was changed later.

## November is named after the Latin word for nine

November was the ninth month of the Romans. *Novem* means nine in Latin. The name remained unchanged when the calendar was changed later.

## December is named after the Latin word for ten

December was the tenth month. *Decem* in Latin means ten. Attempts to change the name happened but the name remained.

## Rainfall can look like a shower when observed from the sky

Precipitation from the clouds in the form of rain is a wonderful sight to look at when observed from the sky. It looks like a localized shower with water pouring from the clouds.

## Mirror neurons explain why humans empathise

Scientists have discovered mirror neurons in the brain. These neurons make the humans act the same way while watching others' action. For example, a person watching a game of football is being played will behave as if he himself is playing it.

## Lemons ripen after you pick them but oranges do not

An orange does not continue to ripen after it is picked. As soon as it is plucked from the tree, it stops ripening. Lemon may turn yellow and ripe from green, even after it is plucked.

## Monday is named after the moon

The old English believed that the moon was the wife of the sun. So there had to be one day in her honour (mōnandæg). Monday was dedicated to the moon.

## Tuesday is named after a Norse God Tyr

The Norse or ancient Germanic people believed in mythologies. They had a god named Tyr who defeated a wolf spirit named Fenrir. But in this process, the hand of Tyr got bitten off. In old English, Tyr is spelled as Tiw and a day was dedicated in his honour (Tiwsdæg), which we know today as Tuesday.

## Wednesday is named after the Germanic God Woden

Woden was the Germanic God who was the god of storms and the father of Tyr. A day was dedicated (Wodensdæg) to him and we know it as Wednesday.

## Thursday is named after the Norse God Thor

Thor was a powerful Norse God, similar to Jupiter of the Romans. He handled the lightning bolts. A day is dedicated to him (Thūresdæg) or Thursday, the day of Thor.

## Friday is named after the Norse Goddess Frigg

Frigg was the wife of Woden, mother of Thor, and goddess of marriage. One day was assigned to her and the English called it Frīgedæg or Friday. The Norse regarded Friday as their lucky day, but the Christians didn't, since Jesus was crucified on a Friday.

## Saturday is named after Saturn

Saturn was the Roman god of sowing. They assigned a day to Saturn and called it *Saturni dies*. The English adopted this and called it Saturday.

## Sunday is named after the Sun

The resurrection of Jesus took place on a Sunday. In 4th century, the church made this day a holiday and forbade everyone to work. The old English spelling is sunnandæg, the day of the sun, an adaptation of the Latin *dies solis*.

## Ancient Romans stuffed a chicken in a duck, in a goose, in a pig, in a cow and cooked them all together

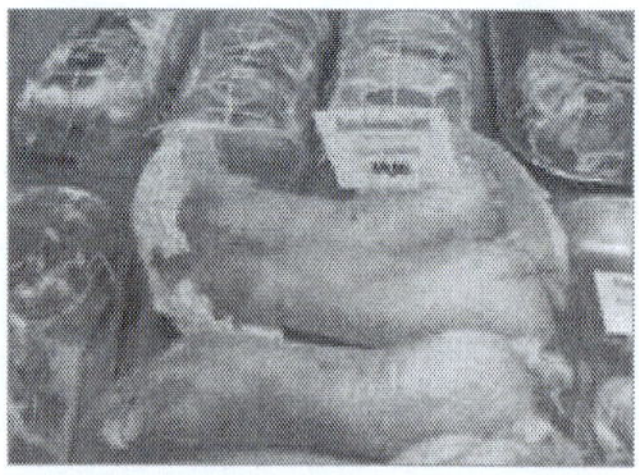

The wealthy Romans liked to eat and invited their friends over for meals. They had slaves who cooked for them. Many complicated meals were cooked, such as a stuffed chicken in a duck, in a goose, in a pig, in a cow cooked all together.

## Pineberry is a strawberry that tastes like pineapples

The pineberry is a mutant form of strawberry, which has white flesh with red seeds. It was discovered by Dutch farmers in France. After six years of cultivation and selection, the commercial varieties were brought under production.

## Al Gore is the only person who is known to have won a Nobel, an Emmy, a Grammy, and an Oscar

Al Gore received the Nobel Peace Prize in 2007 partly for his work in the film *An Inconvenient Truth* (2006). The film won the Oscar for the best documentary. He received a Grammy Award for Best Spoken Word Album in 2009 for his book *An Inconvenient Truth,* and a Primetime Emmy Award for Current TV in 2007.

## Explode means to 'clap off stage'

The word explode is derived from two Latin words *ex* meaning 'out' and *plaudo* meaning 'clap'. In ancient times the bad actors were clapped off the stage by the audience and it was said that 'the actor has been exploded off the stage'.

## Talent means money in Greek

Talent means a natural skill that a person has. It may also mean special aptitude. However, in Greek, talent means a sum of money. It can also refer to property, abilities and powers bestowed upon man.

## Reebok is named after an African antelope

The shoe company Reebok is named after an African antelope rhebok. Reebok is the stylized form of rhebok.

## The first TV remote control was called Lazybones

The first remote control for TV was created by the Zenith Radio Corporation in 1950. It was named Lazybones. It was attached to the TV by a bulky cable. It could turn the TV on and off and also switch channels.

## Karate belts progress from light to dark colour with increasing rank

Karate is a form of martial art that uses a coloured belt to indicate the student's progress. The colour of the belts progresses from white to black. The standard belt colour system is white, yellow, green, brown and black. As the student progressed from the first level to the second, his white belt was dyed to yellow. The process of dying the belt continued with his increasing progress.

## The onion is named after a Latin word 'Unio' meaning a large pearl

The word onion comes to us from the Latin word *Unio*. *Unio* means a large pearl. This could be attributed to the white colour of the single onion bulb. It is believed that the word *Unio* became *Unyon* in English. The onion has various culinary uses and is relished all over the world. Notwithstanding the fact that it brings tears to our eyes, there is an old saying that 'An onion a day keeps the doctor away'.

## Tug of war was once an Olympic sport

From 1900 to 1920, the tug of war was an official sport at the Summer Olympics. The team comprised eight people and a six feet rope. Great Britain won most of the medals with US winning the second most. It is the only game where the winners go backward and the losers move forward.

## A baby kangaroo is so small, it can be kept on a spoon

A baby kangaroo at the time of birth is blind, hairless and only a few centimeters long. Its hind legs are not developed and it uses its forelegs to climb its way through the thick fur on its mother's abdomen into the pouch. At this time, it is so small that it can be scooped up on a spoon.

## Iceland consumes more Coca-Cola per capita than any other nation

Iceland is the biggest per capita consumer of Coca-Cola in the world. It has got a position in the Guinness Book of World Records just for this fact.

# About the Authors

**Dr. Moumita Das** is working as an Assistant Director at National Centre for Innovations in Distance Education (NCIDE), IGNOU. She did her Ph.D. in Botany from the Central Institute of Medicinal and Aromatic Plants, Lucknow. She has several research papers and articles in the areas of medicinal plants, intellectual property rights, and sustainable development in journals of national and international repute. At present, her interest is to identify areas of intervention for devising innovative solutions in the Open and Distance Learning (ODL) system. She has published several articles and papers on the need of innovative interventions in the ODL system.

**Dr. C.K. Ghosh** is presently Director, National Centre for Innovations in Distance Education (NCIDE), IGNOU, New Delhi. He did his Ph.D. as a scholar of Council of Scientific and Industrial Research (CSIR) from The Indian Association for the Cultivation of Science. His Ph.D. topic was 'Electrical, Electro-Thermal and Galvanomagnetic Transport Properties of Thin Solid Films'. He has co-authored five books in Physics and related areas and has more than 80 publications in the form of research papers and articles in several books and journals of national and international repute on the areas of Solid State Physics, Mathematics & Physics Education, Open and Distance Learning and Value Education.

He had been a member of the Board of Management, Academic Council, other Statutory Bodies of IGNOU and several State Open Universities. He has been delivering illustrated talks on diverse topics, some of which are: Science & Technology for Development, Scientific Temper, Frontiers of Astronomy and Astrophysics, Swami Vivekananda's Thoughts on Education, Science in Sports, Innovations in Teaching, Emerging Dimensions of Learner Support in Open and Distance Learning, etc.